The Vegetarian
GOURMET

The Vegetarian GOURMET
Judy Ridgway

Ward Lock Limited · London

First published in Great Britain in 1979
by Ward Lock Limited, 47 Marylebone Lane,
London W1M 6AX, a Pentos Company.

Reprinted 1982

Text filmset in Ehrhardt
by MS Filmsetting Ltd, Frome, Somerset

Printed and bound in Spain
by Editorial Fher S.A.

British Library Cataloguing in Publication Data
Ridgway, Judy
  The Vegetarian Gourmet.
  1. Vegetarian cooking
  I. Title
  641.5′636   TX837

ISBN 0-7063-6176-8 Pbk

The photographs in this book were
taken by Edmund Goldspink. We are
grateful to the following for supplying
accessories for photographs:
Old Bleach Linen; Ravenhead Glass Co;
R&C Vintners and The Redheads.

Line drawings by Gerard Roadley-Battin

Front jacket   *Back jacket*
Ratatouille Roulade and   Artichoke Dip
Glazed Vegetable Pâté   Mexican Dip
                          Indian Curry Dip

Contents

Introduction

The reasons why people turn to vegetarian eating are many and varied. But whatever the reason there is still a need for meals to be both nutritious and appetizing.

So much vegetarian food tends to be bland, dry and extremely uninteresting, and non-vegetarians, not surprisingly, are reluctant to try it. Yet the vegetarian family will want to entertain their non-vegetarian friends and vice versa.

The problem for the first time vegetarian or for those experimenting with the diet is even greater. Their previous cooking experience probably hasn't covered all the alternative protein sources and their friends and relatives may not be convinced about the change. The best advice is probably to go slowly and quietly about the change and only advertise the fact when the results are appreciated.

With *The Vegetarian Gourmet* I have set out to show that with a little care and imagination most cooks can produce delicious vegetarian meals that will appeal to the vegetarian and non-vegetarian alike.

The first two chapters start off with a look at food values and nutrition generally and go on to show how vegetarians can use complementary plant proteins to increase their protein intake. This is followed by a chapter on planning meals in the light of these facts.

Chapter 4 covers all the basic ingredients available to the vegetarian cook; how to prepare them and how to cook them. Dairy produce is included throughout the book though there are both recipes and complete menus which would be suitable for vegans.

The main part of the book includes suggested menus and recipes for everyday vegetarian cooking as well as for dinner parties and gala entertaining. With the exception of Chapters 11 and 12 all recipes are for four people: In Chapter 11 recipes are for twelve people and in Chapter 12 for twenty-four people.

1 Eating Vegetarian

There is no doubt about it – you are what you eat. After all food both liquid and solid is the only source of all the materials that the body needs to keep it in good working order, to grow and to re-build itself. The food you eat not only affects your health but also your personality and your behaviour. If your health is poor and your body is trying desperately to cope with the effects of a bad diet you are unlikely to feel on top of the world and your ability to deal with the ups and downs of everyday life will be impaired. You will probably feel tired and sluggish with a tendency to snap at the slightest provocation.

On the other hand if your body is working well and you feel in peak condition your mental state will usually benefit as well. You will feel much more alert and able to cope.

The connection between health and nutrition is an extremely complicated one. In cases of extreme deficiency there are obvious symptoms of disease such as scurvy in the case of Vitamin C deficiency and beri-beri in the case of Vitamin B deficiency. But in most Western countries the diet is a varied one and on the whole people seem to be reasonably well fed.

Nevertheless, a number of 'new' diseases have appeared or have greatly increased over the last two or three generations and some of them, at least, seem to be related to diet. They include coronary heart disease, obesity and diseases of the bowel.

All these considerations make it extremely important to understand the basics of nutrition – particularly when eating vegetarian means cutting out a substantial source of available food in the form of meat and fish.

Basic nutritional requirements

There are a number of essential materials that the body needs to function properly and these are known as nutrients.

Many of them are found in different sorts of food and in theory it doesn't matter which kind of food you get them from provided that you get them. Others are only available in a limited number of foods and some of these can cause slight problems for vegetarians and even greater problems for vegans who also exclude all dairy produce from their diet.

One of these is iron which, though it is present in eggs, bread and vegetables, is often not in the form that the body can easily absorb. However, this can be overcome by drinking fruit juice which is rich in Vitamin C at the same time as eating the iron containing food. The presence of Vitamin C helps the body to change the iron into a form that can be assimilated more easily.

Another problem nutrient, particularly for vegans, is Vitamin B12. This is thought only to occur in foods of animal origin, particularly liver, kidneys, sardines and herrings. However, the vegetarian can get it from eggs, milk and cheese. But the vegan will have to resort to supplementary tablets of synthesized vitamin.

The essential nutrients are made up of proteins, carbohydrates and fats plus a variety of vitamins and mineral salts.

Proteins

Protein is, apart from water, the largest single constituent of the body. Indeed 17% of the body tissues are made up of protein. So the protein you eat is a major source of material for growth and tissue replacement. At first glance this might seem to be much more important for children than for adults and this is indeed partially the case. But the body is continuously renewing itself and replacing tissues and so adults, too, need a regular supply of protein in the diet. Any excess protein supplied to the body is used as a source of energy and burnt off in activity or stored in the form of glycogen and fat.

Major sources of protein are meat, fish, eggs, cheese, pulses, nuts and seeds. The first two, of course, are not available to the vegetarian, but the alternative sources provide a wide choice of protein-rich food. Minor sources of proteins are bread, cereals, rice and pasta. In fact, almost all food, with the exception of pure fat and pure sugar, contains some protein – even vegetable marrows and cabbage leaves contain protein though these are poor sources of protein percentagewise. However, if you eat enough of them they could contribute significant quantities of protein to the diet.

Of course the various protein sources differ in the type of proteins they provide and these differences affect the amount of useable protein available to the body. These and other factors such as the amount of protein required by the body and theory of complementary proteins are discussed in Chapter 2.

Carbohydrates

Pure carbohydrate is the only nutrient that provides energy alone and contributes nothing else. For this reason, carbohydrates are always blamed as the most 'fattening' of foods. If the body takes in more energy as food than it can use up then the surplus is converted into reserve stores in the unwelcome form of adipose tissue or 'fat'.

However, with the exception of sugar, most carbohydrate foods are extremely useful sources of other nutrients. Two slices of bread, for example, provide a significant proportion of the body's daily protein requirement as well as supplies of calcium, iron and Vitamin B. Wholewheat bread is also an important source of Vitamin E and a variety of minerals. Wholewheat pasta and brown rice are also both useful sources of protein and other nutrients and scrubbed unpeeled new potatoes can contain as much as two thirds of an adult's daily Vitamin C requirement.

Fats

Fats are potentially much more fattening than carbohydrates as weight for weight they can produce about twice the amount of energy. They contain a number of vitamins including A, D, E and K. They are present in a variety of foods such as milk, meat, cakes and herrings as well as being obvious in foods such as butter, margarine and cooking oil.

When fats are eaten they are broken down during digestion into glycerine and fatty acids. These fatty acids are divided into two groups depending on the number of hydrogen atoms in their make-up. Fatty acids having their full quota of hydrogen atoms are called saturated fatty acids and those with four or more hydrogen atoms missing are called polyunsaturated fatty acids.

The latter group contains three fatty acids that the body

is unable to manufacture for itself. These are required for growth and for the healthy development of cells and are therefore known as essential fatty acids. At one time they were incorrectly known as Vitamin F. To date no generally accepted cases have been discovered of anyone suffering from a deficiency of essential fatty acids though some nutritionists believe that such deficiencies are actually more common than is generally appreciated.

The main source of polyunsaturated fatty acids are certain specific vegetable oils such as safflower, corn and soya bean. Minor sources include lean meat and poultry. Saturated fats are found in dairy produce, visible fat on meat, hard margarine and other vegetable oils.

The exact role that each type of fat plays in the body is not fully understood, though it has been suggested that the ratio of the two types of fat consumed in the diet might have a part to play in the incidence of coronary heart disease and this is discussed in more detail later in this chapter.

Most authorities agree, however, that people in the highly industrialized Western societies eat far more fat than their bodies need, either for body building or for energy. In the UK the average person eats about 100–120 grams (about 4 oz) of fat a day which provides 40–50% of the energy in the diet.

Advice offered by medical experts suggest that this percentage should be cut to around 35–40%. More than this would be difficult. Quite apart from the body's needs, fats play an important role in the diet as they carry much of the flavour of foods. They also improve the texture and assist in swallowing by lubricating the food.

Vitamins

Vitamins are present in our food in extremely small quantities yet their absence can cause major deficiency symptoms. The biochemical function of most vitamins in the B group has been discovered, but full details are not known about the functions of Vitamins A, D and E, and there are many gaps in the knowledge about other vitamins.

A brief outline of the current knowledge of the functions of the principal vitamins is given below, together with their vegetarian sources.

Vitamin A
  Aids growth and protects moist tissues like the eyes, throat and lungs.

Found in butter, margarine, carrots, spinach, watercress and apricots.

Vitamin B complex
Assists in converting food into usable materials for body-building or energy.

Found in bread, milk, dairy products, yeast and green leafy vegetables.

Vitamins B1, B2 and niacin are all soluble in water and can be lost in cooking simply by being washed out into the water.

Vitamin C
Aids healing and resistance to infection, and keeps connective tissues in good repair. Aids in the assimilation of iron.

Found in oranges, lemons, blackcurrants, peppers, cauliflower, potatoes, peas, cabbage, spinach and watercress.

Is destroyed to some extent by heat.

Vitamin D
Aids healthy bone development.

Found in margarine, eggs and butter.

Vitamin D can be manufactured in the skin under the influence of sunlight.

Other essential vitamins include Vitamins E and K. The precise role of these vitamins is not really understood but Vitamin E appears to be necessary for a healthy blood circulatory system and Vitamin K is essential for blood clotting. Vitamin E is found in wheat germ and egg yolks, and Vitamin K in green vegetables and soya beans.

Mineral salts
Mineral salts form part of the body structure and they also play a part in the functioning of the enzyme systems that affect all body processes.

Calcium and phosphate form the skeleton and are essential for healthy teeth, bones and muscles. Iron is a constituent of the blood. Other mineral salts required are manganese, magnesium, copper, zinc, potassium, chloride and sulphate. Most of these are needed in such small quantities that dietary deficiencies are thought to be rare.

Iron is found in bread, flour, cereal products and apricots as well as in some vegetables, and as mentioned above, mainly occurs in these sources in a form more easily assimilated in the presence of Vitamin C.

Calcium is present in dairy products and bread; potassium in unpeeled potatoes and lima beans and magnesium is found in cocoa, nuts, soya beans, whole grains and leafy vegetables.

Many people believe that they must eat good red meat to supply all the vitamins and minerals that the body needs. But, in fact, non-meat sources already provide more than half the normal intake of the eleven most frequently cited vitamins and minerals. By stepping up the intake of dairy and vegetable produce to replace meat in the diet the vegetarian is also stepping up his intake of essential vitamins and minerals from these sources and he is unlikely to experience any deficiency.

So what does all this mean in terms of everyday eating? There is no such thing as a perfect diet – rather there are many combinations of different foods that will provide all the nutrients that are required. Chapter 3 contains some guide-lines on planning a balanced diet.

Because of the seeming adequacy of our Western diet, many nutritionists are avoiding the issue by simply advising people to 'eat a little of everything and not too much of anything'. This is fine as far as it goes, but scientists are beginning to understand some of the finer points of healthy eating and it could be that more emphasis will need to be placed on the importance of eating certain types of food rather than others.

Why whole foods?

We are hearing more and more about whole foods these days. Magazine articles frequently suggest recipes using wholemeal flour or brown rice and an increasing number of supermarkets are stocking these products. Health food shops are opening up by the hundreds and even the most conventional nutritionist reluctantly agrees that refining cereals to the extent that is now common practice means that they lose quite a high proportion of their nutrients.

Bread must be the classic example of a food that is refined to a detrimental degree. The British standard white bread loaf contains 70% extraction flour. A United Nations comparison of 100% wholewheat flour and 70% extraction flour shows that with the exception of carbohydrate, which is higher in white bread, all other nutrients are reduced.

	Wholewheat	70% Extraction Flour
Protein per cent in grams	12.2	11.3
Fat	2.4	1.6
Carbohydrate	64.1	72.0
Fibre	2.0	0.1
Thiamin mg per 100 grams	0.37	0.08
Riboflavin	0.12	0.05
Nicotinic Acid	5.70	0.08
Iron	3.50	1.25

This table is by no means exhaustive and the same sort of dramatic reduction occurs with the other vitamins and minerals contained in wholewheat flour.

Admittedly calcium, Vitamin B, nicotinic acid and iron are added to the standard white loaf in an attempt to improve its nutritional value. But this ignores the other missing nutrients as well as the fact that the arrangement of what we eat before we eat it could affect what the body can do with it. Added nutrients may not have the same effect as those naturally contained in food.

Indeed there is serious cause to question all of the additives to our standard loaf and little reason to suppose that they are beneficial. For example, nicotinic acid is still added to bread despite the fact that it is now thought that the nicotinic acid used by the body does not come from cereals at all, but from totally different protein sources.

Nor is the iron added to bread in the easiest form for the body to assimilate which might explain why, after 20 years of adding it to bread, there is no evidence to show it has had any effect whatsoever on the levels of anaemia present in the population!

When wheat is milled and refined to white flour it is the wheat germ and the husk that are lost. The wheat germ contains most of the cereal's nutrients but nutritionists are coming round to the view that the loss of the husk is also detrimental, as the husk is extremely rich in dietary fibre.

Dietary fibre is really all those parts of the food which are not digested by the enzymes in the stomach and intestine and which pass through the system unchanged. It is considered by most experts to be important in the prevention of constipation and indeed of all kinds of digestive complaints from gall stones to diverticulitis. Some researchers are also beginning to think that it might have an important part to play in the prevention of heart disease and cancer.

The name fibre is a bit misleading as foods high in fibre are not necessarily stringy or fibrous. Even 'smooth' foods like bananas contain some fibre. Wholewheat cereals of all kinds are particularly high in fibre content and so are fruit and vegetables, particularly peas, sweetcorn, broccoli and parsnips. Fibre is not affected by cooking so it is not necessary to eat raw food all the time to get sufficient dietary fibre.

If refining flour reduces the nutritional value of bread the same argument holds good for anything made with that flour, whether it is made at home or in the factory. So it is probably worth thinking about buying wholewheat pasta and using wholewheat flour for baking and cooking. Rice is another cereal that loses a high proportion of its vitamin and fibre content when the husk is removed.

The other greatly refined food common in our diet is, of course, white sugar. We need sugar, but this requirement could easily be met by eating other sugar-rich foods, such as fruit. White sugar really doesn't contribute anything to the diet except excess energy and thus excess body fat.

Real brown sugar contains small amounts of potassium and calcium as well as traces of other minerals and vitamins. Molasses, being even less refined, contains the same things in even greater proportions. However, both brown sugar and molasses are still energy producers and they are also thought to be even worse for tooth decay than white sugar.

Honey contains only small quantities of minerals and few vitamins but its constitution is different to the other sweeteners in that it is made up of glucose and fructose – the sugars found in fruit – rather than sucrose.

The various types of sugar seem to play different roles in the body chemistry and these are not really fully understood. They are, however, known to affect blood cholesterol levels and some experts believe that sucrose could be a factor in the incidence of coronary heart disease.

Any discussion on whole foods must touch on the question of additives. Several thousands of chemical substances are currently added to foods during manufacture to pre-

serve and flavour them and to 'improve' their colour and
texture. So far there has been no evidence to show that
anyone has suffered any harm from permitted additives.
But on the other hand there is no proof to the contrary and
the effect could be cumulative. Many processed foods have
their contents printed on the label and the choice is yours.

Some people carry their definition of whole foods beyond
the questions of refining and additives to include only food
which has been grown 'organically' without the use of
artificial fertilizers and hormones. Whether this is a valid
distinction or merely a recipe for lining the pockets of the
specialist growers and distributors is an argument beyond
the scope of this book. However, fresh vegetables from the
kitchen garden do have a flavour that seems to be absent
from those found in most shops.

A question of cholesterol

In recent years there has been considerable emphasis on
the connection between the amount of fat and cholesterol
eaten in the diet, the concentration of cholesterol in the
blood and the incidence of coronary heart disease; with
fats and cholesterol cast as the villains of the piece. Eating
large quantities of foods rich in these items, said the experts,
leads to high levels of blood cholesterol and thence to heart
disease.

This theory was officially endorsed in 1974 by a Department of Health and Social Security Report and again in
1976 by a report of a Working Party set up by the Royal
College of Physicians and the British Cardiac Society.

The second report was even more specific than the first.
The latter contented itself with merely recommending a
general reduction in the intake of fats. But the second report from the Royal College of Physicians put the dietary
blame for coronary heart disease firmly on to saturated
fats.

The Working Party examined evidence from a variety
of sources including population studies and field trials with
dietary changes. The Report stated that conclusive evidence
for any particular dietary regime to reduce the incidence
of heart disease was unlikely to emerge in the foreseeable
future.

Yet despite this statement the report went on to recom-
mend that everyone should not only reduce the overall

amount of fat eaten but that they should replace some of their saturated fat intake with polyunsaturated fats which, it was alleged, would help to counteract any build-up of cholesterol from other sources. The report gave specific details on how to achieve the changeover by cutting down on dairy produce and meat and substituting poultry, fish, soft margarines and oils rich in polyunsaturated fats. The recommended diet was even more stringent for those considered to be at high risk.

The implication for vegetarians of these recommendations are enormous. Dairy produce is a major source of protein, not to mention a variety of vitamins and other nutrients and to cut them out at one fell swoop could lead to serious health problems. Such a diet, of course, is already followed by vegans but considerable knowledge of the food values of vegetable produce is required if they are to remain really healthy.

However, not all authorities agree with the reports quoted and some seriously question the evidence on which they are based. There is a growing body of opinion, backed by authoritative research, which alleges that fats in the diet do not have any causative role in the incidence of heart disease and that eggs and dairy produce are not harmful in normal quantities.

There are a number of reasons why cholesterol was thought to be a causative factor in heart disease. First it has been known for a long time that arteries which are showing signs of hardening contain large amounts of fats in the build up of materials in the hardening walls and subsequent research showed that these fats included a high level of cholesterol.

Secondly, patients who suffer from heart disease frequently have higher than average levels of blood cholesterol. Thirdly, high blood cholesterol levels and hardening of the arteries may be induced in experimental animals by feeding them with lots of fat. Fourthly there is known to be a definite connection between the amount of animal fat consumed and the level of cholesterol in the blood. Taking all these factors together it is easily concluded that a reduction in animal fat intake should reduce the probability of suffering from hardening of the arteries.

However, recent research in Aberdeen, Scotland has shown that cholesterol is not present at the start of the hardening process and many distinguished research workers who previously believed cholesterol to be a causative factor are changing their views. Some researchers go even further and state that the cholesterol present at the later stages might be the result of a repair function of cholesterol.

In addition, meticulously controlled trials of cholesterol reducing diets carried out both in Great Britain and in the United States over the last ten years – surprisingly ignored by the Royal College of Physician's Working Party – have failed to produce any difference in the recurrence of heart disease or in the ultimate death-rate of patients. In each of the trials the blood cholesterol was lowered quite significantly and if it had been a causative factor, a beneficial result would have been expected.

Advocates of the polyunsaturated fat diet state that there are no known disadvantages to the diet and that it might possibly be of help. However, it seems rather drastic to change the dietary habits of centuries on the basis of such poor evidence. There is also growing evidence to support the suggestion that lowering the blood cholesterol levels could increase the incidence and frequency of gall stones. After all cholesterol does have a number of essential functions in the body. These concern the absorption of fats into the blood stream and their transport to different parts of the body.

To carry out the latter function, cholesterol combines with fats in the blood to form two substances known as high-density lipids and low-density lipids. Recent research suggests that it is the ratio of these two substances in the blood that is the more useful index of the risk of developing coronary heart disease. And this ratio is not related to the type of fat in the diet. However, it is affected by smoking, exercise levels and obesity – all known to be important factors in heart disease – and by the amount of carbohydrates in the diet.

Even more recent research has found evidence that a high intake of dietary fibre from cereals reduces the likelihood of suffering from coronary heart disease, though the mechanism behind this remains unexplained.

So it now looks as if there is no need to rush off to follow the rather drastic advice contained in the Report published by the Royal College of Physicians. However, we do eat far more fat than we need. So if you have even the slightest weight problem it makes sense to cut down on fats of all kinds as well as on carbohydrates and to step up the amount of exercise you take so that you more nearly balance your energy intake and output on a daily basis.

The energy balance

To some people the pulses and cereals of a vegetarian diet sound like a recipe for overweight. To others the emphasis on vegetables seems like the road to starvation. Of course, neither of these extreme pictures is correct. All the food we eat provides essential nutrients and energy, and vegetarians are merely substituting one set of food patterns for another. There is no intrinsic reason why they should get fatter or thinner than others provided that they get their energy balance right. In fact surveys have shown that despite the seemingly high carbohydrate content of the diet, vegetarians and vegans are less likely to be fat than meat eaters.

Fatness or obesity is a real problem in the Western world and it is not just the looks of the obese person that are at stake. Obesity increases the risk of diabetes, heart disease, gout, high blood pressure, bronchitis, gall stones and varicose veins. Fat people have a higher accident rate and they die younger.

According to figures collected by the American Society of Actuaries, a man over 45 who is 11 kg [25 lb] overweight reduces his life expectancy by 25%. If he loses his excess weight his life expectation returns to normal. All very cogent reasons for trying to keep one's weight down.

There is usually no intrinsic reason why a person should be overweight provided that the energy balance is maintained. The energy balance is quite simply the difference between energy input in the form of food and energy output in the form of activity. If these are balanced the body weight will remain constant. If, however, the energy input is too high, some of it is not used up in activity and this will be stored in the form of body fat. If the energy input is too low the body starts to use up whatever store of fat it happens to have.

Different foods vary in their energy content. This is measured in Calories and food such as butter, margarine, cream cheese and cooking oils are extremely high in Calories. Next come biscuits, cakes, sugar, dry cereals, nuts, cheese and double cream, closely followed by eggs and bread. Most fresh fruit and vegetables are fairly low in Calories. Meat and fish fall in the middle sections of the range, so removing them from the diet and substituting cheese and eggs makes little difference to the input side of an individual's energy equation.

But how much input do we need? First of all energy is required to maintain the fundamental processes of life. The heart must be kept beating, the body temperature maintained and the organs kept functioning. This requirement is called the basal metabolic rate (BMR) and is measured when a person is resting. Surprisingly, even if someone stayed in bed all day a healthy person would still need two thirds of their normal intake. The actual BMR varies with age and sex but the average adult needs about 1,600 Calories just to cover these basic needs. However, there is considerable variation between individual rates and people of the same sex, age and size can differ by as much as 30%.

The BMR is constant for any particular individual but the rest of his energy requirements will depend on his activity. People doing heavy work or taking a lot of exercise need to take in more energy than those in sedentary occupations. And here again actual requirements to sustain particular activities vary by hundreds of Calories. For this reason any average guidelines for energy requirements can only give a rough indication of what is needed. However, here are some examples of the total daily Calorie intake that are recommended for various age groups and types of people. These figures are compiled from the Ministry of Agriculture, Fisheries and Food Manual of Nutrition.

Age	Males Calories	Females Calories
Under 1 year old	800	800
3 years old	1,600	1,600
8 years old	2,100	2,100
15 years old	3,000	2,300
20–50 (active life)	3,000	2,500
20–50 (inactive life)	2,700	2,100
65 years old	2,300	2,000
over 75	2,100	1,900

The trick then is to balance the energy equation but unfortunately nothing is really known about how this is done.

Some people are hearty eaters yet rarely put on weight. Others may get fat not because they are excessive eaters but because their energy expenditure is so low that they are still eating more than they are using.

The simple remedy for overweight is to eat less and exercise more. But this is easier said than done. Actually, exercise is most effective in helping to keep weight down in the first place. And remember that eating less means eating less in terms of Calories. It's no good cutting out bread and potatoes only to drown your other vegetables in melted butter. Nor does eating less mean near starvation. A diet containing less than 1,400 Calories probably won't contain all the nutrients required to keep the body healthy.

Food reform

Nutrition is usually taken to be concerned with maintaining health and preventing disease. However, despite the doubts of the orthodox medical profession, some doctors and nutritionists have taken the connection between food and health to its logical conclusion and have studied the effects of diet on a wide variety of diseases. As a result some of them have not only recommended specific diets to cure particular diseases but have achieved cures with these diets. Others have studied food allergies – an area that an increasing number of experts agree can affect the health of the individual concerned.

Some of the studies have also led to development of food reform diets for healthy people as well as for those with particular illnesses. Most of them include whole foods and many of them are vegetarian.

It is not possible here to review all of them but perhaps one of the most interesting and influential is the Bircher-Benner system developed earlier this century by Dr M. O. Bircher-Benner in his Swiss clinic. Among many other ideas he has been responsible for the introduction of the now almost universally popular muesli.

Dr Bircher-Benner's system was developed for invalids and those poor in health through painstaking tests and clinical experience. It is designed to help them regain their fitness and vitality. This research also led to the development of a basic diet for fit people to help them avoid disease by increasing resistance and to help them combat the illnesses of old age.

It is largely, though not wholly, a vegetarian diet, avoiding meat, fish and eggs except as accessory foods or on isolated occasions and cuts out all stimulating drinks such as tea, coffee and alcohol.

Dr Bircher-Benner came to the conclusion that it was the deterioration of food that takes place during cooking and other processing that was at the root of many bodily evils and his recommendations include a directive to eat at least half the daily energy intake in the form of raw food, to start each meal with raw food and to eat green leaves every day.

Many of the things which Dr Bircher-Benner fought for have become a matter of general acceptance today. He recognized the value of vitamins long before many of his contemporaries and his ideas continue to find a hearing long after his death in 1939. An excellent book on his approach to nutrition is *Eating Your Way to Health* by Ruth Bircher.

2 Making the most of Plant Proteins

Protein food has traditionally been regarded as the most important part of the diet and in the UK this protein food has usually been meat. It takes pride of place at each meal with the rest of the food subordinate to it. But meat is only one of the many sources of protein. The task facing the vegetarian is to choose a variety of alternative protein rich foods that will do the same job that meat is popularly held to do so well.

Of course, much of the importance placed on protein food is justified in that it is the great body builder without which we would certainly waste away. So how much do we need and does it make any difference what kind of protein food we eat?

The protein controversy

First of all the basic question that divides many nutritionists is 'how much is enough?' This question is an extremely difficult one to answer as people vary tremendously both in their individual requirements and in their needs in different circumstances.

There are official recommended daily intake levels for all nutrients published by the Department of Health and Social Security. The recommended levels on these proteins take into account energy output levels. They state, for example, that the recommended daily intake of protein for a moderately active 35–65 year old man is 70 grams or about 3 oz; and 55 grams or just over 2 oz for a woman of the same age. These quantities may appear to be very low but remember that protein foods are not made up purely of protein and it may be necessary to eat more than double these amounts of protein foods to get the recommended amount of pure protein.

Set out below are some more recommendations from the Department of Health and Social Security:

Children	Boys	Girls
1–2 years	30 g	30 g
3–5 years	40 g	40 g
7–9 years	53 g	53 g
9–12 years	63 g	58 g
12–15 years	70 g	58 g
15–18 years	75 g	58 g

Men	18–35	35–65	65–75
Sedentary	68 g	65 g	59 g
Moderately active	75 g	73 g	
Very active	90 g	90 g	

Women	18–55	55–75
Most occupations	55 g	51 g
Very active	63 g	48 g
Pregnant	60–68 g	

However, these figures really do not help the individual very much as they are average figures. They have also been adjusted upwards to take into account the fact that the actual minimum protein requirement would be considered unacceptable in Great Britain.

The recommended daily intake of protein is worked out by plotting the results of experiments on a distribution curve. About the same number of people require less than average as require more, and the majority of people fall within 20% above and below the average. The recommended daily average is taken as the higher figure, i.e. the average plus 20%.

This means that there should only be a very small number of people whose needs are not met by the recommended figure. But it also means that some people could consume 40% less than the recommended figure without being deprived in any way. But there is no way of knowing where in the distribution curve a particular individual lies.

The matter is even further complicated by the fact that a person's requirements varies with the ordinary stresses and strains of everyday life. Loss of sleep, minor infections, pain and anxiety can all cause one's protein requirement to leap by more than a third. Proteins are lost from the body even more quickly after operations, burns and accidents and so the body's requirement is even greater during convalescence.

Orthodox nutritionists agree that in this country most people eating a general, mixed diet probably get more than enough protein. But there are some experts who believe that the recommended levels are too low. They argue that to maintain vigour and youthfulness as long as possible, it is necessary to supply the body with quite large quantities of protein and that this high level should be increased to 150 grams [5½ oz] or more daily after periods of low intake or after disease. On the other hand dieticians such as Dr Bircher-Benner believe that 50 grams [2 oz] is nearer to the ideal daily intake.

Deficiency in protein is not easy to detect. The development of protein malnutrition is a slow and gradual process and the first stages are quite undetectable. The issue is also complicated by the fact that the body seems to be able to adapt to lowered protein intake levels. But whether there is any adverse long term effect is not known.

Nor is it any good looking around you to see what others are successfully eating as this will tell you nothing about your own requirements. The only answer seems to be to try and develop a kind of 'body wisdom' based on the condition of your body such as nail and hair growth, whether or not cuts and sores heal quickly and how you feel in terms of energy levels and general health.

Animal or vegetable?

Meat, usually thought to be the great protein provider, is not in fact the richest source of protein. In fact it ranks somewhere in the middle of the percentage quantity scale with around 25% protein in its make up. Soya flour is actually the most concentrated natural source of protein, containing almost half its weight in protein.

Next come certain cheeses such as Parmesan, which is 36% protein. Meat follows with fish, nuts, beans, peas and lentils in the same category. At the lower end of the scale are the cereals and eggs at around 10% and milk at about 4%, though dried skimmed milk contains 34% protein. Vegetables are also near the bottom of the scale.

However, it is not just the quantity of protein contained in food that decides how useful it will be in body building. If it were, vegans and vegetarians would not need to be concerned about protein levels and there would be no controversy about preferable protein sources. After all most dairy produce and many plant proteins have an excellent showing on the quantity scale.

However, all proteins are not the same. The protein in milk differs from that in cereals and the protein in liver is different to that in soya beans. But all of them are made up of a combination of the same 22 amino acids. These amino acids are released into the blood stream during digestion and they are carried to wherever they are needed to be reassembled into body proteins.

Some amino acids are produced naturally in the body. But eight of them are not and for the building of new body proteins to continue these eight essential amino acids must be provided from proteins eaten in the daily diet. In addition they need to be present simultaneously and in the right proportions, otherwise protein synthesis will fall to a very low level. The other amino acids in foods are also used in body building but they are not considered to be essential, as the body can, if necessary, manufacture them for itself.

All the essential amino acids are present in most foods, but unfortunately they do not necessarily occur in the ideal proportions for the body to use. There are usually one or more amino acids present in disproportionately small quantities. This means that if half the ideal proportions of one of the essential amino acids is missing from a protein then the body can only use half the total quantity of all the other essential amino acids present, the rest is wasted or used to supply energy. It also means that twice the amount of that protein would need to be eaten to fulfil daily requirements. The most deficient amino acid is called the limiting amino acid.

The highest quality proteins would be those in which there was no limiting amino acid and all the protein was usable by the body. In practice the total amount of protein eaten is never fully usable by the body but the protein in eggs comes very near to it. In fact, animal proteins occupy the highest rungs on the usability scale and for this reason they used to be classed as first class proteins. However, meat is not at the top; milk, cheese and fish are all higher up the scale.

Some vegetable proteins approach the level of meat and these include soya beans and whole rice. The rest of the nuts and pulses are in the 40–60% usability range and this of course means that it would be necessary to eat rather a lot of them to cover daily requirements because of the limiting amino acids waste. This is an important consideration in a vegan diet.

For vegetarians the situation is very much easier. Dairy produce is high on the usability scale and some of them – dried skim milk and Parmesan cheese for example – are also high on the percentage quantity scale too. Contrary to popular belief it doesn't look as if vegetarians are likely to miss out in the protein stakes.

Complementary proteins

However, it would be a pity to dismiss plant proteins out of hand – they are cheap and plentiful and add great variety to the diet. The trick is to eat proteins that have mutually complementary amino acid patterns i.e. one protein that is low in one particular amino acid is matched with a protein that is rich in the same amino acid. In this way the protein value of the meal is increased in such a way that the whole is greater than the sum of the parts. This is because the matching of amino acids means that more of each protein is available for use by the body. Such protein mixes do not result in a perfect protein but they can increase the protein quantity by as much as 50% above the average of the items eaten separately.

Many people unconsciously take advantage of this complementary effect. Bread and cheese for example complement each other very well, the cheese filling in the bread's lysine and isoleucine deficiencies. Baked beans on toast is another example. Here the combination of wheat and beans can increase the amount of usable protein by up to 33%.

So what are the most effective combinations?

1) Milk products and grains

Dairy products have excellent usability ratings and they thus make good supplements to any foods. But they are particularly rich in two amino acids and as we saw with the bread and cheese example, combine particularly well with cereals which are low in the same two amino acids.

You don't need to add much of the milk product to increase the protein quality quite substantially. Two tablespoons of non-fat dried milk, for example, added to 100 g [4 oz] wheat or rye flour increases the protein quality by about 45%.

The same amino acid strengths mean that dairy products

also complement the proteins in nuts and seeds. So that cheese and peanuts or milk and sesame seeds make good combinations.

2) Pulses and grains
The proteins in pulses and grains have almost exactly opposite strengths and weaknesses and therefore complement each other well. The addition of milk can add even more to the protein quality of these combinations.

3) Pulses and seeds
A similar situation occurs with the amino acids of pulses and nuts and seeds. Once again dairy produce can help to fill the amino acid gaps in nuts and seeds and a good mixture is peanut butter with milk for sauces.

Much more detailed information on complementary proteins and the proportion in which they should be mixed is given in *Diet For a Small Planet* by Frances Moore Lappe.

Here is a guide to the amount of usable protein in average servings of some of the various protein foods eaten by vegetarians.

Food	Total Weight	Total Grams of Protein	Weight of Usable Protein
Dairy Produce			
Cottage cheese	100 g	17 g	13 g
Milk non-fat dry solids	25 g	10 g	8 g
Parmesan cheese	25 g	10 g	7 g
Milk	100 g	9 g	7 g
Yogurt	100 g	8 g	7 g
Cheddar cheese	25 g	7 g	5 g
Edam cheese	25 g	8 g	6 g
Pulses			
Add 5% if complemented			
Soya beans (dry)	50 g	17 g	10 g
Broad beans (dry)	50 g	13 g	6 g
Kidney beans (dry)	50 g	12 g	5 g
Chick peas (dry)	50 g	11 g	5 g
Lentils (dry)	50 g	13 g	4 g

Nuts and Seeds
Add 2–3% if complemented

Sunflower seeds	25 g	7 g	4 g
Peanuts	25 g	8 g	3 g
Cashew nuts	25 g	5 g	3 g
Sesame seeds	25 g	5 g	3 g

Grains and their Products
Add 2–3% if complemented

Pasta	150 g	5 g	3 g
Oatmeal	50 g	4 g	3 g
Brown rice	75 g	5 g	3 g
Wheatgerm	12 g	3 g	2 g
Bread, wholewheat	1 slice	2.4 g	1.2 g
Soya bean flour defatted	138 g	65 g	40 g
Soya bean flour full fat	138 g	52 g	32 g
Wholewheat flour	120 g	16 g	10 g

A final point to note is that all protein whether of high or low quality is only used efficiently if there is sufficient energy in the diet. Theoretically the daily requirement of protein could be supplied by six eggs. But if these were eaten alone the low energy/Calorie content would mean that most of the amino acids would be diverted away from repair work to supply energy. This means that high protein diets should be looked at with care as they may not be doing the job they are designed to do.

On the other hand most protein foods contain fats and carbohydrates as well as protein in their make up and this will affect their Calorie contribution to the body's energy balance. It does not mean, however, that such protein foods are necessarily fattening. Cheese, for example, has a high fat content but because the protein in cheese is of such a high quality only small quantities are required to fulfil daily requirements. Nuts on the other hand do have very high calorie to usable protein ratios. Incidentally, one of the least fattening high protein foods is cottage cheese, closely followed by skim milk and buttermilk.

3 Planning Balanced Menus

Planning balanced menus involves selecting the right balance of different types of food to build up and maintain good health. But it also involves selecting food that tastes delicious and looks attractive. There is no point in producing an extremely healthy meal if it looks unattractive and un-appetizing. The digestive juices will not work so well and your family or friends could well be put off the idea of healthy foods permanently.

Nor will they want to eat the same things – however nutritious – day in and day out. Variety is extremely important and here the judicious use of fresh foods in season, the freezer and your imagination can help to ring the changes.

Planning the day for a balanced diet

Ideally each meal in the day should contain some of all the essential nutrients and certainly they should all appear at some time during the day. This is because many of them are not stored in the body and therefore need to be supplied regularly. In addition if protein is not eaten with an energy source then it will be used to provide energy rather than to rebuild the body tissues.

Few foods are made up of only one nutrient and conversely no food contains all the nutrients we need. But of course we don't really think of eating nutrients – it's food that we enjoy at mealtimes. Perhaps the easiest way to plan a balanced diet is to divide food into categories according to its major attributes and then to choose something from each group for each meal. Set out below are four groups of food selected as specially good sources of particular nutrients.

1) Eggs, cheese, milk, pulses and nuts:
   Supply protein, B group vitamins, Vitamins A and D and minerals.
2) Bread, cereals, rice and pasta:
   Supply carbohydrates for energy, Vitamin E, minerals and fibre. They can also add to the protein supply.
3) Cooking and salad oil, butter, cream, margarine:
   Supply fats for longer term energy and Vitamins A and D.
4) Fruit and vegetables:
   Supply Vitamins A, B group and C, minerals and fibre.

The traditional pattern of breakfast, lunch and dinner probably fulfils the nutritional requirements as well as any, though there is some disagreement about the relative weight of the various meals. Some experts would have you eat like a king at breakfast, a prince at midday and a pauper in the evening. Others suggest a light breakfast and supper with the main meal of the day at midday.

However, this is not a convenient pattern for everyone and some people are forced to eat their main meal in the evening. This should not cause too many problems so long as the meal is not eaten so late that the digestive process interferes with sleep patterns and provided that a good breakfast is eaten before going to work.

Unfortunately, nowadays many people start the day on a hastily consumed cup of tea and maybe a piece of toast or some cereals. Others do without breakfast altogether. Yet breakfast really is an essential start to the day. Many authorities believe that breakfast should provide at least a quarter of your daily food intake. After all breakfast usually follows a fast of anything up to twelve hours and that is far longer than any other gap between meals in the twenty-four hour cycle.

First thing in the morning the body's blood sugar level is at its lowest and breakfast provides the essential nutrients when they are needed most. It is the amount of sugar in your blood that determines the amount of energy you can produce and this in turn affects how you think and act throughout the day.

Studies in Great Britain and the United States show that the omission of breakfast results in poorer scholastic performance in school children and in higher accident rates for foundry workers and lorry drivers.

Slimmers are major offenders when it comes to skipping breakfast as this seems an easy way of cutting down on overall food intake. But this can lead to cheating through hunger at mid-morning or over-eating at lunch time. It is actually far better to eat small meals at regular intervals throughout the day.

Planning individual meals

As well as fulfilling nutritional and health requirements, a meal should be an enjoyable pastime and there are a number of simple factors which can really make a difference to the appeal and taste of a meal.

The first of these is the choice of flavourings to be used. This is a particularly important consideration for vegetarian food which too often tends to be insipid or bland. Of course, nuts, pulses and cereals do have a flavour of their own but these can often be greatly enhanced by the careful choice of flavourings. So it is important to experiment with flavourings. But don't go mad on the latest discovery and use it in every dish. The same herb or spice in the main dish, sauce and starter would become extremely monotonous.

Texture, too, is important. It is not good dietetically, nor does it make an interesting meal, if there is more than one dish prepared and finished in the same way. Several dishes made with pastry or deep-fried would be boring. So it's best to vary the textures by serving crunchy vegetables with light soufflés and smooth dishes, a creamy sauce with pastry dishes and rice or potatoes with casseroles.

The look of the food can also set the taste buds working. So mix colours as well as textures and avoid food that is all white or all brown. Arrange the food attractively on serving dishes or individual plates and use garnishes to improve its appearance. Parsley, crumbled egg yolk, tomatoes, watercress and roasted nuts are all effective and you can easily experiment with other things.

In Great Britain we are used to three course meals with a central course consisting of a main dish with vegetables. However, the emphasis can shift a little with vegetarian meals. Sometimes the dishes will all have equal weight. But do make sure there aren't too many rich or fatty dishes in the same meal. This can be both over-facing and bad for the digestion.

One final point concerns the balance of raw and cooked

foods. To some extent this will depend on your own in-
clinations and convictions. But it is a fact that fresh raw
food often contains more of its original nutrients. This is
because some vitamins are destroyed by heat and others are
leached out into the cooking liquor and this is often thrown
away.

Dr Bircher-Benner suggested that a raw food dish should
be used to start every meal and this is a convenient method
of making sure that you have a regular intake of raw foods.
Other people like to eat at least one raw food or salad meal
each day. But whatever style of eating you choose, do make
sure that you don't overcook your food – particularly
vegetables and that you don't leave chopped or grated raw
food exposed to the air – both sure ways of losing much of
their goodness.

Making the most of complementary proteins

Perhaps the most important thing to remember when using
plant proteins is that your daily protein requirement need
not necessarily come from one large important item in the
two main meals of the day. In fact it is much more likely
that it will come from the sum total of all the protein-
containing foods eaten during the day.

It is an easy step from the realization of this fact to
making a conscious effort to enhance the protein value of
particular dishes either by adding extra protein-rich ingredients or by making use of the complementary protein
theory.

The three most effective combinations of protein foods
outlined in Chapter 2 were milk products and grains;
pulses and grains; and pulses and seeds. Set out below are
some good examples of these combinations and some hints
on putting them into practice.

Milk products and grains
Cereals with milk: *muesli*
Bread and cheese: *sandwiches*
Cheese and rice: *rissoles and patties*
Milk, cheese and cornmeal: *polenta*
Milk and wheatflour: *sauces*
Cheese and pasta: *baked casseroles*

Try adding milk, cream or yogurt to potato dishes. The

greater the amount of the milk product the better the overall protein value.

Use non-fat dried milk with grains and pulses. Don't bother to dilute it – just add it in its dry state.

Pulses and grains
Beans and wheatflour or bread: *baked beans on toast*
Peas and beans with rice: *risotto*
Beans and corn: *vegetable casseroles*

When using pulses and rice the best combination from a complementary protein point of view is about 3:1 grains to pulses. If the recipe calls for a higher ratio of beans, add some milk products or seeds.

Use soya flour in cakes and pastries to give a nice short texture as well as to increase the protein content. Soya flour can also be added to bread and pancakes. Use to replace flour on a 7:1 ratio.

Add soya flour to pâtés, terrines and rissoles.

Pulses and seeds
Chick peas and sesame seeds: *Houmous*
Beans and nuts: *terrines and pâtés*
Beans and sunflower seeds: *vegetable stuffings*

All bean dishes are enhanced proteinwise by the addition of a milk product. Serve butter beans in white sauce or red beans with cottage cheese and herbs.

Add nuts and seeds to salads and to vegetable dishes.

Add protein to desserts by including soya flour or ground nuts in crunchy toppings and in pastry.

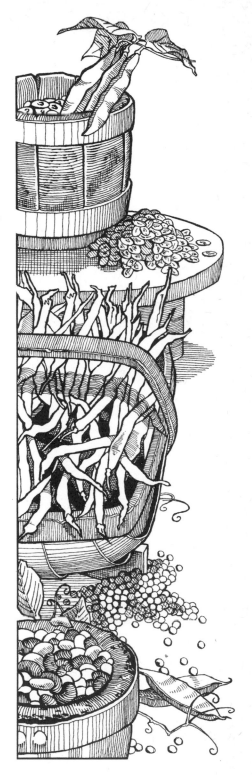

4 Ingredients and Basic Preparation

The majority of ingredients used in the menus and recipe sections are to be found in most large supermarkets and much of it is everyday produce on sale all over the country. Even foreign vegetables like aubergines and peppers can be bought in most towns nowadays, and courgettes and asparagus are both fairly easy to come by in season and they are both available deep frozen.

A few items such as buckwheat, fennel and sesame seed and some of the more exotic beans will require a visit to a specialist grocer or to the local health food store. And it's probably sensible to stock up with things like tinned chestnuts, artichoke hearts and flageolet beans when you happen to see them.

With the cereals my own inclination is for wholewheat flour and pasta, brown rice and the like. Many of these are now available in ordinary shops and supermarkets, so it isn't necessary to do all your shopping at the health food shop unless you want to.

Herbs and spices are particularly important in vegetarian cookery, so stock up with them. If you have a garden grow as wide a variety as you can. Use them fresh in summer and dry them for the winter months.

Basic equipment

There is a common misconception that vegetarian cookery takes ages to prepare – all that chopping and grinding! But this isn't really the case. However, all good cooking takes some time to prepare, so a careful selection of useful equipment can help to cut down preparation time.

The vegetarian cook doesn't really need much in the way of extra equipment, though a mechanical or electric grater is a big help if you are keen on salads and a pressure cooker dramatically cuts the time that beans take to cook. So plan your kitchen in the normal way, adding some of the items listed below depending on the type of food you like to prepare and the size of your pocket.

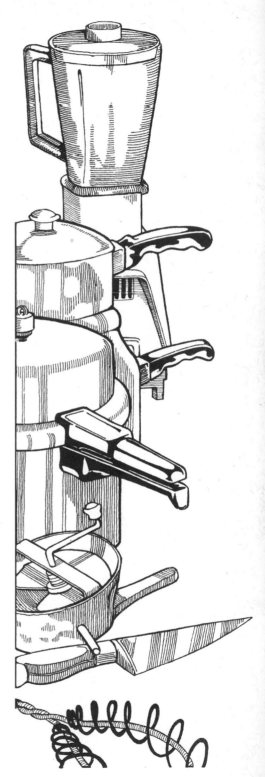

    French cook's knife – your basic tool for most dishes

    Mechanical or electric grater

    Blender/liquidizer with grinder attachment

    Mouli-mill for soups and purées – gives a coarser texture than the liquidizer

    Pressure cooker

    Double boiler

    Two or three stainless steel steamers to fit inside your pans

    Wire whisk for sauces

A good set of pans is really worth investing in. Go for stainless steel – with a copper base if you can afford it. Alternatively enamelled cast iron is fine though you should get rid of it if it chips. Many people believe that aluminium is dangerous and copper kills any vitamin C that remains during cooking. A thick base spreads the heat – particularly important for top of the stove cookery.

Some recipes suggest that the dish is cooked 'au bain marie'. The simplest way to do this is to fill a roasting tin with about 5 cm [2 in] water and place the dish to be cooked in this.

The store cupboard

A store cupboard is always useful and this is particularly true for the vegetarian cook. Some items require advance cooking. It's no good rushing out to buy black eye beans, for example, the day you want to eat them for unless you have a pressure cooker they won't be ready until the next day. Other items such as herbs and spices are in constant demand and need to be on hand.

Here's a check list of most of the items I keep in my own store cupboard.

Herbs

    Thyme, marjoram, basil, sage, summer savory, rosemary, tarragon, chives, dill weed, chervil, oregano, bay leaves, mint, parsley, fennel and dill seed, celery seed and celery salt.

Spices

    Allspice, ground cumin seed, caraway seeds, turmeric, cardamoms, coriander, cloves; ground, root and stem

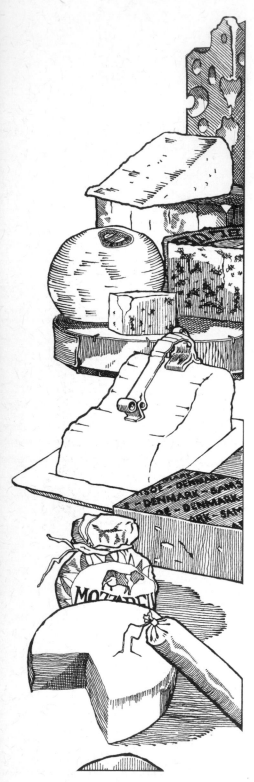

ginger; nutmeg and mace, cinnamon, curry powder, mixed spices; black, white, Cayenne and paprika pepper; sea salt.

Flavourings and sauces

Vanilla and almond essence, garlic and garlic salt, tomato paste, Marmite or Barmene, French and English mustard, Worcestershire sauce (not for strict vegetarians), cider and wine vinegar and tomato ketchup.

Nuts, pulses and seeds

Peanuts, almonds, walnuts, cashew nuts, hazelnuts, peanut butter, sesame seeds, soya flour, lentils and a selection of dried peas and beans.

Cereals

Plain and self-raising flour, fine and medium oatmeal, rolled oats, buckwheat, flaked barley, flaked millet, muesli mix, yellow cornmeal, rice and a selection of pasta.

Preserves and sweeteners

Home-made jams, chutneys and pickles, honey, molasses, Barbados sugar, demerara sugar, a little caster sugar for special desserts, and a selection of dried fruits.

Miscellaneous

Baking powder, cream of tartar, bicarbonate of soda, agar-agar, gelozone, non-fat dried milk powder and a selection of tinned foods for standbys and luxuries.

Cheese

For really strict vegetarians it is probably worth noting that cheeses made with vegetarian rennet are available at most health food stores and some supermarkets.

Apart from tinned foods, avoid buying too much of any one item unless you are really sure you will get through it quickly. There's nothing worse than looking at a mountain of beans or spaghetti and wondering if you will ever come to the end of it. These items do deteriorate over time so they are best eaten fresh.

Basic preparation

Some of the items used in the recipes could be unfamiliar. So here's a run down on basic preparation.

1) Pulses

In general dried pulses need to be soaked before cooking. This can be done overnight in cold water. Alternatively the process can be speeded up by pouring boiling water over the pulses and leaving them for about 2 hours before cooking. However, this does tend to split the skins.

Lentils: No soaking required. Simmer for about 30–45 minutes depending on how 'mushy' you like them.

Split peas: No soaking required. Simmer for about an hour.

Pinto, Borlotti and Greek Foulia beans: Soak overnight in cold water. Simmer for an hour then start to check the softness of the beans. If left too long they will start to fall.

Chick peas, whole green peas, haricot beans, black eye beans and butter beans: Soak overnight in cold water. Simmer for about $1\frac{1}{2}$ hours and then start checking.

Red kidney beans and soya beans: Soak overnight in the fridge. Soya beans tend to start fermenting if left in a warm kitchen. It is important to *boil* the soaked beans for at least 10 minutes before adding them to oven-cooked dishes. If cooking the beans in a slow cooker, they should be boiled as above before adding them to the other ingredients in the cooker and cooking them for 4 hours. Even when fully cooked, soya beans tend to retain a slight 'bite'.

Always add salt at the end of cooking as salt seems to make the beans harder to soften.

The pressure cooker will at least halve the amount of time required to cook beans. Use plenty of water and experiment to find ideal times.

2) Wholemeal flour

All recipes have been tested with wholemeal flour but they all work just as well with white flour. I do not find that there is usually any need to change the proportion of ingredients when using wholemeal flour in place of white flour. However, some people prefer to use 80% extraction flour for cakes and pastry as this gives a smoother texture. The degree to which the flour has been milled will also affect the texture of the finished dish.

Here are one or two pointers to bear in mind when using wholemeal flour.

a) Pastry made with wholemeal flour tends to be extremely crumbly and can be difficult to roll out. This can be overcome either by adding a little more water than usual or by pressing the pastry into the pie dish without

rolling it out. The latter method is particularly useful for sugar pastry made with wholemeal flour.

b) Sauces made with wholemeal flour look a little speckled. This is due to the bran in the flour and this can be sieved out if preferred. A roux sauce is made by melting butter over a low heat and stirring in the flour. Cook the mixture for 2–3 minutes and then gradually add the liquid, stirring all the time. Bring to the boil and cook for a few minutes. A panada is a particularly thick roux sauce.

c) Wholewheat pasta behaves in almost exactly the same way as white pasta and ravioli dough made with wholemeal flour rolls out extremely well.

3) Polenta
Use a wire whisk when adding cornmeal to boiling water. This helps to prevent lumps forming. If the mixture does go lumpy just pass through a sieve and continue as instructed. This note also applies to semolina and rice flour recipes.

4) Brown rice
All the recipes in the book have been tested with brown rice. This takes a little longer to cook than polished rice and has a nutty flavour. It does not need to be washed after cooking as the grains remain separate.

5) Sesame seeds
Unless they are being used for decoration, sesame seeds are usually ground before use. They are thought to be much more digestible used in this way. To toast them, sprinkle whole sesame seeds into the base of the grill pan and place under the heat for 2–3 minutes until brown in colour. Do not allow them to burn. Grind and store in an air-tight jar.

6) Nuts
Nuts are usually cheaper if bought whole in their brown skins and these are usually removed before use. To remove skin shake peanuts in a bag, rubbing slightly at the same time. Hazelnuts will need 5 minutes in the oven before shaking or rubbing the skins loose. Almonds should be placed in a pan of boiling water for a minute or so, after which the skins are easily removed.

7) Dried fruits

Raisins, currants, dates and sultanas are used as they are bought. Dried bananas can be used soaked or unsoaked. Dried apricots, prunes, peaches, apples and pears need soaking overnight in cold water. Wash the fruit first and then use the water in which the fruit has been soaked to cook them in.

8) Dairy produce

I have used butter for testing all the recipes but there is no reason why a good margarine should not be used instead.

9) Vegetarian stock

There are three types of stock available to the vegetarian and the choice of these will depend on the strength and flavour required for the particular recipe. They are made as follows:

a) Vegetable water saved from simmering, steaming or baking vegetables. This can be kept for a few days in the fridge or stored for longer periods in the freezer. Try freezing some in ice-trays; the cubes can then be stored in polythene bags in the freezer and small quantities used for baking more vegetables or for sauces.

b) Specially prepared strong stock can be made by boiling one large sliced onion, one sliced carrot, a stick of celery, bayleaf and parsley and thyme in a pint of water for about an hour. Strain and use or store.

c) A vegetable extract such as Marmite or Barmene dissolved in water makes an excellent standby stock or the extract can be added to a) and b) above to give added colour and strength.

10) Setting agents

Gelatine is, of course, of animal origin and strict vegetarians will not want to use it. However, if you do use it remember to mix with a little cold water first before adding hot water to dissolve it. The gelatine should not be boiled.

Agar-agar is one vegetarian alternative. It gives a really clear jelly and is made by sprinkling into boiling liquid and stirring vigorously until completely dissolved. Particular care is needed to make sure it does not go lumpy. If it does it can be strained. Agar-agar starts to set very quickly after removing from the heat, so use at once.

Gelozone is another vegetarian alternative to gelatine. It

must always be made into a smooth paste with cold water
and then brought to the boil and simmered for 2–3 minutes.

11) Bean sprouts

Bean sprouts are on sale in a number of shops these days
but it is a very simple matter to sprout your own. Sprouting
at home also means that you have a much wider choice of
sprouts – some seed merchants offer as many as a dozen
different varieties.

The choice ranges from the mung bean of the familiar
Chinese beanshoot, through to alfalfa seed and spicey
fenugreek to special mixtures devised by the seed merchants. Don't try to sprout beans that have been sitting
around your store cupboard for the last six months.

Sprouts are particularly rich in protein as well as in
essential vitamins and minerals. They also contain dietary
fibre and a number of enzymes which help in digestion.
They are about the freshest vegetable you are ever likely to
have as they are still growing when you eat them. Even
fresh garden vegetables lose 25% of their vitamins within
30 minutes of being picked.

Sprouting is extremely easy. All you need to do is to
place a small amount of the seed or beans in a large jar and
cover the neck with a piece of muslin or gauze. Next fill the
container with tepid water and shake well to clean the seed.
Repeat this three times and then leave the container on its
side so that the water will drain away.

Fill the jar with more tepid water every morning and
every evening for about 4–6 days, making sure that the
water can drain away easily. Don't let the sprouts grow too
big or they will lose their flavour and nutritional value.

Sprouts are best eaten raw, but they can be lightly
steamed or sautéed. But do make sure not to over cook
them. Excess sprouts store well in the fridge in a closed
polythene container.

Freezing vegetarian food

The freezer is just as useful to the vegetarian cook as it is to
the general cook. The way you use it will of course depend
on your life-style and on the kind of food that you and your
family prefer. However, there are some things that it is
extremely convenient to have readily available in the fridge.
These include:

Cooked rice
Cooked beans of various kinds
Grated cheese
Breadcrumbs
Pastry
Fruit purées
Batter and pancake mixes
Bread and rolls
Basic sauces
Fresh herbs
Grated orange and lemon rind
Stock

It's a good idea to freeze vegetable stock in ice-cube containers and then store in polythene bags. This means that you can use as little or as much stock as you require.

Remember, too, that some things do not freeze well. These include eggs in their shells, hard-boiled eggs in any form, mayonnaise and nutmeg. Most spices take on a rather more peppery or ginger flavour and vanilla can develop a very unpleasant taste if kept frozen for too long. Curry, too, gets stronger after a while and most sauces tend to thicken up. Mashed potato freezes well, but sliced or cubed potatoes in soups and stews tend to fall making the finished dish rather cloudy. It is, therefore, probably better to add the potatoes when the dish has been reheated prior to serving.

Textured vegetable protein

Textured vegetable protein (TVP) is now available in a variety of forms, ranging from plain, unflavoured chunks, slices and mince to canned varieties emulating the classic dishes of English, French and Italian cuisine. Most of it is based on soya beans.

TVP is very much a matter of personal taste. It can be very economical and is nutritionally excellent. However, I prefer my beans to look and taste like beans and so I have not included any recipes for TVP.

Using dietary supplements

Here again we are back into the realms of controversy. Most orthodox nutritionists state that dietary supplements are not really necessary for most people in the UK as our diet is sufficiently varied. Other experts believe that the modern diet is lacking in various elements and that these deficiencies should be made good by the addition of items such as wheat germ and brewer's yeast and vitamins. Certainly natural supplements such as these are unlikely to do you any harm and they could be extremely valuable. The trouble is that on the whole they are not very palatable though enthusiasts state that you gradually get used to the flavour. However, quite often they can be mixed in with other ingredients to mask the flavour. Items to consider are:

1) Brewers' yeast powder
This is rich in vitamins of the B complex as well as having relatively high protein content. One level tablespoon will provide 2 grams of usable protein or around 5% of your total daily requirements. The amino acid pattern also makes it a good complementary mix for nuts and cereals.

2) Wheat germ
This has a similar protein content to Brewers' Yeast and is rich in Vitamin E. Though its general level of vitamins and minerals is nothing like as good.

3) Wheat bran
This can be added to soups and cereals to improve the fibre content of the diet.

5 The Main Meal of the Day

Stuffed Onions with Rosemary

Potato Stew with Spiced Red Cabbage and Green Beans

Bananas in Honey

Stuffed Onions with Rosemary

Steam onions and allow to cool slightly. Remove centres from onions and chop finely. Mix with ground beans, rosemary and seasoning. Spoon back into the centres of the onions. Place onions on a heatproof plate and dot with butter. Place under the grill and cook for 5–8 minutes until well browned.

4 large or 8 small onions
100 g [4 oz] ground cooked soya beans
1 teaspoon rosemary
salt and pepper

Potato Stew

Finely slice onions and fry in cooking oil until golden. Add oatmeal and continue cooking for a few minutes. Then add stock and Marmite. Bring to the boil, stirring from time to time and add chopped potatoes and seasoning. Simmer for 30 minutes until potatoes are cooked, adding a little more stock if the stew gets too thick. Serve sprinkled with a little grated cheese if desired.

4 large potatoes
4 onions
4 tablespoons fine or medium oatmeal
1 tablespoon Marmite or yeast extract
625 ml [1¼ pints] vegetable stock
cooking oil
salt and pepper
grated cheese (optional)

Spiced Red Cabbage

1 small red cabbage
15 ml [1 tablespoon] vinegar
45 ml [3 tablespoons] stock
2 cloves
5 ml [1 teaspoon] Worcestershire
    sauce
$\frac{1}{4}$ teaspoon cinnamon
$\frac{1}{4}$ teaspoon nutmeg
salt and pepper

Slice red cabbage and place in a thick based pan. Mix stock, vinegar and Worcestershire sauce. Add spices and seasoning and pour over the cabbage. Bring to the boil and simmer for 45 minutes or until cabbage is soft.

Bananas in Honey

4 bananas
2 tablespoons honey
juice of 1 lemon
knob of butter

Melt butter in a frying pan. Add honey and lemon juice. Quickly sauté peeled and halved bananas in this mixture. Serve with remaining liquid poured over the top.

Cream of Leek Soup

Fennel Bean Pot with Potato Cakes and Endive Salad with Onion Dressing

Orange Slices with Pears

Cream of Leek Soup

450 g [1 lb] leeks
1 tablespoon English mustard
    powder
1 medium onion
25 g [1 oz] butter
75 ml [3 fl.oz] cooking sherry
625 ml [1$\frac{1}{4}$ pints] vegetable
    stock
$\frac{1}{2}$ teaspoon sugar
salt and pepper

Garnish
mustard and cress

Melt butter in pan and add chopped onion. Sauté until golden. Add chopped leeks and continue to cook for 3–4 minutes. Add cooking sherry and bring to the boil. Add all other ingredients and bring to the boil again. Simmer for 45 minutes and rub through a sieve or mouli. Correct seasoning and reheat. Garnish with heads of mustard and cress.

Fennel Bean Pot

Soak beans overnight. Finely slice onions and garlic and fry in a little cooking oil until golden. Add beans and mix with fennel seed, chervil and seasoning. Transfer to an earthenware casserole dish and pour on red wine. Cover and bake at 190°C/375°F/Gas Mark 5 for 1½ hours. Increase temperature to 200°C/400°F/Gas Mark 6 for a further 40–45 minutes. Stir from time to time.

50 g [2 oz] haricot beans
50 g [2 oz] black eye beans
50 g [2 oz] butter beans
50 g [2 oz] Borlotti beans
2 onions
2 cloves garlic
250 ml [½ pint] red wine
½ teaspoon fennel seed
½ teaspoon chervil or parsley
cooking oil
salt and pepper

Potato Cakes

Peel and boil potatoes until soft. Mash with butter and milk and mix in flour and seasoning. Press out on a greased baking tray to about ¼ in thick. Mark into sections with a knife. Bake at 200°C/400°F/Gas Mark 6 for 40–45 minutes until slightly crisp and brown. Serve with butter.

450 g [1 lb] potatoes
4 tablespoons plain flour
50 g [2 oz] butter or margarine
45 ml [3 tablespoons] milk or
  stock
salt and pepper

Endive Salad with Onion Dressing

Wash curly endive and tear into pieces. Mix with thinly cut slices of red and green pepper. Mix dressing ingredients with finely chopped onions and pour over the salad. Serve at once.

½ head curly endive
¼ green pepper
¼ red pepper

Dressing
60 ml [4 tablespoons] salad oil
30 ml [2 tablespoons] cider
  vinegar
4 spring onions or ¼ small onion
black pepper

Sliced Oranges with Pears

Peel and slice pears and oranges and arrange alternately in a dish. Squeeze third orange and pour the juice over the fruit. Chill and serve with whipped cream.

2 oranges
2 pears
juice of 1 orange

Guernsey Salad
Dutch Pea Soup with Nut Dumplings
Apples Stuffed with Raisins and Honey

Guernsey Salad

8 tomatoes
45 ml [3 tablespoons] sour cream
10 ml [2 teaspoons] lemon juice
1 tablespoon freshly chopped
   mint
salt and pepper
lettuce

Skin the tomatoes and roughly chop. Mix sour cream, lemon juice, seasoning and mint. Arrange tomatoes in individual dishes on a bed of lettuce. Spoon the dressing over the top.

Dutch Pea Soup

225 g [8 oz] split green peas
2 large onions
1 teaspoon Marmite or yeast
   extract
sprinkling of nutmeg
salt and pepper
water
cooking oil

Soak peas overnight in water. Drain and make the liquid up to 1 litre [2 pints] with more water. Slice onions and brown in cooking oil. Add peas, water, Marmite and a sprinkling of nutmeg. Season and bring to the boil. Simmer for about $1\frac{1}{2}$ hours. Purée and serve with Nut Dumplings.

Nut Dumplings

25 g [1 oz] breadcrumbs
25 g [1 oz] ground peanuts
30 ml [2 tablespoons] milk
1 egg
a little self-raising flour
salt and pepper

Soak breadcrumbs in milk. Add the peanuts and egg and beat well. If the mixture is too runny to form into balls add flour to make a stiffish paste. Season and shape into 20 small dumplings about 1 cm [$\frac{1}{2}$ in] in diameter. Drop into soup or into boiling salted water and cook for 5–8 minutes. Serve with soup.

Apples Stuffed with Raisins and Honey

4 cooking apples
4 tablespoons raisins
4 teaspoons honey
1 teaspoon cinnamon

Wash and core apples and cut round the centre to stop the skin splitting. Dust raisins with cinnamon and stuff into the centre of the apples. Top with a teaspoon of honey on

each apple. Bake in a fairly hot oven for about 45 minutes–
1 hour, 200°C/400°F/Gas Mark 6.

Grapefruit and Orange Salad

Polenta Tomato Casserole with Jacket Potatoes and Baked Leeks

Apple Crunchy Pudding with Custard

Grapefruit and Orange Salad

Peel and slice 2 grapefruit and 1 orange and divide into 4 bowls. Squeeze the remaining orange and pour over the fruit. Chop the sprigs of mint and sprinkle over the top and place an olive in the centre of each dish. Serve chilled.

2 grapefruit
2 oranges
4 sprigs mint
4 black olives

Polenta Tomato Casserole

Bring water to boil and pour in corn meal stirring all the time. Add salt and butter and continue stirring until mixture thickens. Continue cooking on a low heat for 20–30 minutes, stirring regularly. The finished mixture should be thick and smooth. Add Parmesan and nutmeg and correct seasoning. Pour into a basin and allow to cool and set. Meanwhile make a roux sauce with the remaining butter, flour and milk and season to taste. Slice cold polenta into thin wedges and layer in a casserole dish with finely sliced onions and tomatoes. Sprinkle with remaining Parmesan and top with sauce. Finish off with breadcrumbs and a little more nutmeg. Bake in a moderate oven 190°C/375°F/Gas Mark 5 for 30–40 minutes.

Polenta
100 g [4 oz] yellow corn meal
750 ml [1½ pints] water
50 g [2 oz] butter
50 g [2 oz] Parmesan cheese
½ teaspoon salt
¼ teaspoon nutmeg

Sauce
50 g [2 oz] butter
50 g [2 oz] flour
375 ml [⅔ pint] milk
salt and pepper

Other Ingredients
3 onions
4 large tomatoes
50 g [2 oz] Parmesan cheese
25 g [1 oz] breadcrumbs

Baked Leeks

4 medium leeks
4 tablespoons frozen peas
a little rosemary
salt and pepper

Wash and slice leeks and layer in a casserole with frozen peas. Add herbs and seasoning and cover. Bake in a moderate oven 190°C/375°F/Gas Mark 5 for 1 hour.

Apple Crunchy Pudding

700 g [1½ lb] cooking apples
25 g [1 oz] Demerara sugar
25 g [1 oz] bran flakes
a little water

Peel and slice apples. Simmer with a very little water and purée. Place in the base of an ovenproof dish. Mix Demerara sugar and bran flakes and sprinkle on the top of the apple purée. Bake at 200°C/400°F/Gas Mark 6 for 30 minutes.

Tomato, Cauliflower and Tarragon Soup with Wholemeal Rolls

South American Baked Eggs with Steamed Broccoli and Vichy Carrots

Pear and Ginger Crumble Pudding

Tomato, Cauliflower and Tarragon Soup

225 g [8 oz] cauliflower
225 g [8 oz] tomatoes
1 medium onion
1 oz butter
75 ml [3 fl.oz] cooking sherry
625 ml [1¼ pints] vegetable stock
1 teaspoon dried tarragon
½ teaspoon sugar
salt and pepper

Melt butter in pan and add chopped onion. Sauté until golden. Add cooking sherry and bring to the boil. Add cauliflower, tomatoes, vegetable stock, sugar, tarragon and seasoning. Bring to the boil and simmer for 45 minutes. Rub through sieve or mouli. Correct seasoning and reheat. Serve sprinkled with a little more tarragon.

Wholemeal Rolls

Warm water to blood heat and mix 3–4 tablespoons with the dried yeast. Leave in a warm place for about 10 minutes until creamy. Sift flour and salt and keep in a warm place. Mix flour, water and yeast mixture and knead in the bowl for 5–10 minutes. Shape into rolls and place on a greased baking tray. Cover with a cloth and leave in a warm place to rise to double their size (about 1 hour). Bake in a hot oven 230°C/450°F/Gas Mark 8 for 10–12 minutes. Test if the rolls are ready by rapping the base with your fingernails. It should sound firm.

450 g [1 lb] wholemeal flour
325–350 ml [13–14 fl.oz] warm water
1 teaspoon salt
12 g [½ oz] dried yeast

South American Baked Eggs

Finely chop onions and green pepper and fry in cooking oil until the onions are transparent. Mash beans with a fork and mix with onion mixture. Add thyme and seasoning and spoon into an ovenproof dish. Make four wells in the mixture and break an egg into each one. Pour over the wine and bake at 220°C/425°F/Gas Mark 7 for about 15–20 minutes or until the eggs are set.

4 onions
1 green pepper
325 g [12 oz] cooked red beans
4 large eggs
60 ml [4 tablespoons] red wine
1 teaspoon thyme
cooking oil
salt and pepper

Vichy Carrots

Peel and slice carrots and place in a pan. Cover with stock and add all remaining ingredients except parsley. Bring to the boil and simmer for 20 minutes. Turn up the heat and continue cooking until all the liquid has been used up and the carrots are coated with the glaze. Turn into a heated dish and sprinkle with parsley.

450 g [1 lb] carrots
25 g [1 oz] butter
1 tablespoon soft brown sugar
vegetable stock
salt and black pepper
finely chopped parsley

Pear and Ginger Crumble Pudding

Peel, core and slice pears and chop ginger. Melt butter in a pan and add your favourite muesli mix and sugar. Place half the pears and ginger in an ovenproof dish and cover with half muesli mixture. Repeat these two layers and pour on the water and a little ginger syrup. Bake in a moderate oven 180°C/350°F/Gas Mark 4 for 1 hour. Serve hot or cold with fresh cream or yogurt.

700 g [1½ lb] pears
50 g [2 oz] butter
100 g [4 oz] muesli mix
50 g [2 oz] Barbados sugar
90 ml [6 tablespoons] water
1 piece of stem ginger and a little syrup

Country Vegetable Soup
Spinach Ravioli with Tomato Salad
Chocolate Mousse

Country Vegetable Soup

450 g [1 lb] mixed vegetables:
  carrots, leeks, potatoes,
  celery and turnip
2 onions
25 g [1 oz] butter
750 ml [1½ pints] vegetable stock
1 teaspoon Marmite or yeast
  extract
1 bay leaf
½ teaspoon marjoram
¼ teaspoon thyme
salt and pepper

Melt butter in pan and gently fry chopped onion. Add remaining vegetables roughly chopped and continue to fry for a further 5 minutes. Add stock, Marmite, herbs and seasoning. Bring to the boil and simmer for 1 hour. Rub through a sieve or mouli. Correct seasoning and reheat.

Spinach Ravioli

Pasta
350 g [12 oz] plain flour
4 eggs
15 ml [1 tablespoon] oil
salt

Filling
1 medium onion
1 clove garlic
225 g [8 oz] grated cheese
275 g [10 oz] spinach
125 ml [¼ pint] red wine
¼ teaspoon nutmeg
salt and pepper
cooking oil
2 litres [4 pints] salted water
50 g [2 oz] melted butter
50 g [2 oz] Parmesan cheese

Put the flour and salt in a bowl. Make a hollow in the middle and add the oil and eggs. Mix well with a fork to form a dough. Roll out, fold in half and replace in the bowl. Leave for 1 hour. Meanwhile finely chop onion and garlic and fry for 5 minutes in cooking oil. Add wine and simmer for 20 minutes. Season with salt, pepper and nutmeg and add washed spinach. Cook for about 5 minutes. Remove from heat and add cheese, stirring well. Unfold pasta and roll out thinly. Cut into 4 cm [1½ in] squares and place a teaspoonful of the spinach mixture in the centre of half the squares. Place a square of pasta on top of each, sealing the edge well with water. Bring water to boil and add salt. Cook the ravioli in the salted water for 10 minutes. Remove with a draining spoon and place on warmed plates. Pour over melted butter and sprinkle with Parmesan cheese. Serve immediately.

Tomato Salad

Peel and slice tomatoes and slice cucumber. Place in a bowl with marjoram and seasoning. Add oil and vinegar well mixed and chill for $\frac{1}{2}$ hour.

4 large Mediterranean tomatoes
10 cm [4 in] cucumber
1 teaspoon marjoram
60 ml [4 tablespoons] olive oil
30 ml [2 tablespoons] wine
    vinegar
salt and pepper

Chocolate Mousse

Melt chocolate over hot water with a little water to achieve a creamy consistency. Separate the egg yolks from the whites and mix with chocolate. Whisk egg whites with a pinch of salt until really stiff. Add to chocolate mixture and pour into individual pots and place in fridge to set. Just before serving sprinkle with flaked almonds.

100 g [4 oz] plain chocolate
3 eggs
a little water
flaked almonds
pinch of salt

Shropska

Courgette and Oatmeal Savoury with Buttered Potatoes and Salad in Season with Lemon Dressing

Orange Semolina Pudding with Marmalade Sauce

Shropska

Coarsely chop all vegetables and layer in individual bowls. Top with salt and pepper, grated cheese and lemon juice. Chill for 30–45 minutes.

4 large tomatoes
1 small onion
$\frac{1}{2}$ green pepper
10 cm [4 in] cucumber
3 sticks celery
100 g [4 oz] grated cheese
juice of 1 lemon
salt and pepper

Courgette and Oatmeal Savoury

2 large onions
450 g [1 lb] courgettes
4 tomatoes
cooking oil
4 tablespoons medium oatmeal
75 g [3 oz] cheese
4 eggs
250 ml [½ pint] vegetable stock

Finely chop onions and fry in cooking oil until golden in colour. Add oatmeal and continue cooking for 2–3 minutes. Add seasoning and stock stirring all the time. Continue cooking for 10 minutes until mixture thickens. Meanwhile fry courgettes in oil until half cooked and peel and slice tomatoes. Place in an ovenproof dish. Beat eggs and add to oatmeal mixture. Stir in most of the cheese and pour over the vegetables. Top with remaining cheese. Bake at 190°C/375°F/Gas Mark 5 for about 45 minutes. Check the centre is cooked through with a fork before serving.

Lemon Dressing

60 ml [4 tablespoons] salad oil
30 ml [2 tablespoons] lemon
   juice
1 teaspoon French mustard
½ teaspoon sugar
1 teaspoon finely chopped onion
1 teaspoon finely chopped
   parsley
black pepper

Place all ingredients in a bowl and beat well with a fork. Pour over the salad.

Orange Semolina Pudding with Marmalade Sauce

Pudding
50 g [2 oz] semolina
750 ml [1½ pints] milk
25 g [1 oz] butter
30 ml [2 tablespoons] milk
grated orange rind

Sauce
2 tablespoons orange marmalade
juice of 1 orange
15–30 ml [1–2 tablespoons] water

Place semolina in a pan with milk, butter and honey and slowly bring to the boil, stirring all the time. Simmer for 10–15 minutes and add grated orange rind. Serve in individual bowls.

    To make sauce, place all ingredients in a pan and slowly heat through. Pour over the semolina and serve at once.

Mixed Pulse Soup with Herb Bread

Jerusalem Eggs, Braised Celery and Steamed Carrots with Breton Tomato Salad

Baked Apples Seville

Mixed Pulse Soup

Soak peas and beans overnight. Drain, then cook the beans as directed in Chapter 4. Place them in a pan with all the other ingredients except green vegetables and slowly bring to the boil. Simmer for 1–2 hours until all the vegetables are soft. 15 minutes before serving add green vegetables. Blend or sieve and serve with freshly chopped parsley sprinkled on top.

50 g [2 oz] dried red beans
25 g [1 oz] chick peas
25 g [1 oz] lentils
1 onion
750 ml [1½ pints] water
50 g [2 oz] green vegetables –
   spinach, cabbage or lettuce
1 teaspoon chopped mint
¼ teaspoon ground cumin
pinch of tumeric
salt and pepper
freshly chopped parsley

Herb Bread

Soften butter and mix with herbs. Slice the French loaf into eight slices. Butter each slice with the herb butter and press back into a loaf shape. Wrap in foil and bake at 230°C/450°F/Gas Mark 8 for about 5 minutes.

1 short French loaf
50 g [2 oz] butter
½ teaspoon mixed herbs
½ teaspoon thyme
½ teaspoon basil
½ teaspoon rosemary

Breton Tomato Salad

Wash and slice chicory and lay on a serving plate. Skin and slice tomatoes and place on top of the chicory. Sprinkle with black pepper. Mix yogurt, lemon juice and sorrel and pour over the tomatoes. Garnish with a little more fresh sorrel around the edges. If fresh sorrel is not available use 2 tablespoons young spinach leaves.

4–6 Mediterranean tomatoes
2 heads chicory
60 ml [4 tablespoons] yogurt
10 ml [2 teaspoons] lemon juice
½ teaspoon sugar
1 tablespoon finely chopped
   fresh sorrel or spinach
black pepper

Jerusalem Eggs

8 hard-boiled eggs
450 g [1 lb] Jerusalem artichokes
450 g [1 lb] potatoes
75 g [3 oz] butter
50 g [2 oz] flour
250 ml [½ pint] milk
salt and pepper

Peel and steam Jerusalem artichokes for about 10 minutes until cooked through. Boil potatoes and mash with 25 g [1 oz] butter, three quarters of artichokes and salt and pepper. Halve eggs and remove yolks and mash with remaining artichokes. Season and pile back into egg whites. Place in the base of a casserole dish. Melt remaining butter and make a roux sauce with the flour and milk and season to taste. Pour over the eggs. Spoon the potato and artichoke mixture round the edge of the dish and bake at 220°C/425°F/Gas Mark 7 for 20 minutes.

Braised Celery

2 celery heads
1 onion
1 teaspoon Marmite or yeast
    extract
100 ml [4 fl.oz] hot water
salt and pepper

Wash and trim celery heads. Cut in half and lay lengthways in a fireproof dish. Finely slice onion and lay on top of celery. Dissolve Marmite in hot water and pour over the vegetables. Season and bake in a moderate oven 180°C/350°F/Gas Mark 4 for 20 minutes then raise temperature as for Jerusalem Eggs and continue cooking.

   If the celery is to be cooked on its own bake for 1 hour at original temperature.

Baked Apples Seville

4 cooking apples
12–16 dates
2 tablespoons Seville orange
    marmalade
4 teaspoons ground almonds,
    hazelnuts or peanuts
cider

Wash and core apples. Cut round the centre to stop the apples splitting during cooking. Stuff with dates, ground almonds and marmalade. Top with a little cider and bake at 220°C/425°F/Gas Mark 7 for ¾ hour.

Chick Peas à la Greque

Stuffed Potatoes with Tomatoes

Coffee Ice Cream

Chick Peas à la Greque

Soak chick peas overnight and boil in water for about 1½ hours until almost cooked. Fry finely sliced onions in cooking oil until transparent. Add mushrooms, halved or quartered according to size. Drain chick peas and add to mushroom mixture. Pour over the wine and add all other ingredients. Bring to the boil and simmer for 30 minutes. Serve chilled.

100 g [4 oz] chick peas
2 small onions
100 g [4 oz] mushrooms
2 teaspoons tomato paste
½ teaspoon oregano
1 bay leaf
500 ml [1 pint] white wine
salt and pepper
cooking oil

Stuffed Potatoes with Tomatoes

Scrub the potatoes and score the skins. Boil for 30 minutes in salted water. Drain and leave to cool. Slice the bottom off each potato so that it can stand unsupported. At the other end scoop out enough potato so that in the hollow there is enough room to hold an egg. Grease an ovenproof dish and place the potatoes on it. Wash the tomatoes and cut a cross on the top of each. Place them between the potatoes. Flake half the butter and dot over the vegetables. Lightly season and sprinkle with a little of the cheese. Break an egg into each potato. Now add the rest of the cheese and a little milk to each potato. Season again. Sprinkle with paprika and add the rest of the flaked butter. Bake at 220°C/450°F/Gas Mark 8 for 20 minutes.

8 large, round potatoes
4 tomatoes
50 g [2 oz] butter
salt and pepper
100 g [4 oz] grated Emmental cheese
8 small eggs
30 ml [2 tablespoons] milk
paprika
parsley

Coffee Ice Cream

Whip milk and cream until stiff. Whisk eggs until thick and pale in colour. Add instant coffee and whisk some more. Quickly fold into cream mixture and spoon into a container. Freeze at once.

3 eggs
1 tablespoon runny honey
125 ml [¼ pint] double cream
75 ml [3 fl.oz] milk
3–4 teaspoons instant coffee

Leeks Vinaigrette

Barley Broth, French Bread, Spinach and
Watercress Salad

Grapefruit Ice Cream

Leeks Vinaigrette

6–8 medium leeks
1 small onion
fresh parsley

Dressing
90 ml [6 tablespoons] salad oil
30 ml [2 tablespoons] cider
   vinegar
$\frac{1}{4}$ teaspoon French mustard
$\frac{1}{4}$ teaspoon sugar
salt and pepper

Steam, wash and coarsely chop leeks for about 8–10
minutes. Allow to cool. Finely slice onions and mix with
leeks in individual bowls. Mix dressing and pour over leeks
and onions. Sprinkle with finely chopped parsley.

Barley Broth

1 large onion
50 g [2 oz] flaked barley
25 g [1 oz] pearl barley
50 g [2 oz] lentils
1 small tin baked beans
1 litre [2 pints] vegetable stock
thyme and bay leaf
salt and pepper
cooking oil
fresh parsley

Finely chop onion and fry in cooking oil for about 5 minutes
to soften. Add barley and lentils and pour on the stock.
Sprinkle with herbs and seasoning and add baked beans.
Bring to the boil and simmer for $1\frac{1}{2}$–2 hours. Serve sprinkled
with fresh parsley.

Spinach and Watercress Salad

225 g [$\frac{1}{2}$ lb] small spinach leaves
$\frac{1}{2}$ bunch watercress
60 ml [4 tablespoons] oil and
   lemon dressing
$\frac{1}{2}$ teaspoon sweet basil and
   summer savory

Wash spinach and watercress. Shred and mix. Toss in
dressing and herbs.

Grapefruit Ice Cream

Whip all ingredients together until as stiff as possible. Spoon into a container. Cover and freeze.

250 ml [½ pint] double cream
150 ml [6 fl.oz] grapefruit juice
150 g [6 oz] sugar

Tomato Pasta Salad with Marinated Mushrooms

London Loaf with Buttered Green Beans and New Potatoes

Coriander Apples

Tomato Pasta Salad

Cook pasta in boiling salted water. Just before the pasta is cooked add frozen peas. Continue cooking for five minutes. Mix oil, vinegar, tomato paste and seasoning. Drain pasta and peas and pour tomato dressing over the top. Leave to cool. Chop onion and celery finely and shred green pepper. Cube cheese. Mix all ingredients together and garnish with fried bread croûtons and chopped parsley.

100 g [4 oz] pasta
½ onion
3 sticks celery
¼ green pepper
50 g [2 oz] grated cheese
4 tablespoons frozen peas
2 tablespoons tomato paste
30 ml [2 tablespoons] salad oil
15 ml [1 tablespoon] vinegar
½ teaspoon oregano
salt and pepper
fried bread croûtons
chopped parsley

Marinated Mushrooms

Mix lemon juice, oil, tomato ketchup, thyme and crushed clove of garlic. Finely slice mushrooms and pour over the marinade. Sprinkle with salt and black pepper. Leave to stand for 1–2 hours before serving.

450 g [1 lb] mushrooms
30 ml [2 tablespoons] lemon juice
60 ml [4 tablespoons] salad oil
15 ml [1 tablespoon] tomato ketchup
1 teaspoon thyme
1 clove garlic
salt and black pepper

London Loaf

75 g [3 oz] breadcrumbs
150 g [6 oz] mixed nuts
　　(peanuts, hazelnuts and
　　almonds)
2 onions
6 tomatoes
2 carrots
100 g [4 oz] mushrooms
4 sticks celery
150 ml [6 fl.oz] vegetable stock
2 eggs
25 g [1 oz] ground sesame seeds
　　(optional)
$1\frac{1}{2}$ teaspoons ground cumin
$\frac{1}{2}$ teaspoon celery seed or celery
　　salt
4 tablespoons freshly chopped
　　parsley
salt and pepper

Finely chop all vegetables and mix with dry ingredients, herbs, spices and seasoning. Bind with beaten eggs and stock. Press into a baking tin approximately 30 × 20 cm [12 × 8 in]. Bake at 200°C/400°F/Gas Mark 6 for 1 hour. If desired serve with tomato sauce.

Coriander Apples

4 Bramley cooking apples
200 ml [8 fl.oz] cider
2 teaspoons honey
2 teaspoons Barbados sugar
$\frac{1}{2}$ teaspoon coriander

Dissolve honey and sugar in cider. Peel, core and slice apples and lay in a fireproof dish. Sprinkle with coriander and pour over the sweetened cider. Cover and bake for 30–40 minutes at 200°C/400°F/Gas Mark 6. Serve with fresh cream or custard.

6 Cold Meals and Salads

This chapter includes twelve full menus and a selection of twelve individual salad recipes.

Asparagus with Fresh Mint and Sour Cream Sauce

Sliced Peanut Loaf with Beanshoot and Onion Salad,* and Green Potato Salad and Tomatoes

Peaches in White Wine

Asparagus with Fresh Mint and Sour Cream Sauce

Steam asparagus, drain and allow to cool. Mix sour cream with mint and seasoning. Arrange asparagus on individual plates and cover the tips with sauce.

450 g [1 lb] asparagus (fresh or frozen)
1 small carton sour cream
1 tablespoon freshly chopped mint
salt and pepper

Sliced Peanut Loaf

Finely chop onions, mushrooms and tomatoes and add all other ingredients except oatmeal. Mix well and roll in oatmeal. Shape into a loaf and place on a greased tray. Bake at 180°C/350°F/Gas Mark 4 for 45 minutes–1 hour. Allow to cool and serve sliced.

100 g [4 oz] mushrooms
3 onions
2 tomatoes
2 tablespoons peanut butter
50 g [2 oz] ground peanuts
50 g [2 oz] soya flour
50 g [2 oz] breadcrumbs
2 eggs
2 teaspoons dill weed
salt and pepper
25 g [1 oz] oatmeal

* See page 73.

Green Potato Salad

350 g [12 oz] potatoes
1 head chicory
1 small bunch chives
watercress
4–6 Cos lettuce leaves

Dressing
90 ml [6 tablespoons] oil
45 ml [3 tablespoons] wine vinegar
1 teaspoon French mustard
a little sugar
salt and black pepper

Cook potatoes and dice hot. Mix dressing and pour over warm potatoes. Leave to cool and add chopped green salad items just before serving.

Peaches in White Wine

4 peaches
250 ml [½ pint] white wine
1 tablespoon honey
5 ml [1 teaspoon] lemon juice
¼ teaspoon mixed spices

Place wine, sugar, lemon juice and spices in a pan and bring to the boil. Continue boiling for 5 minutes. Turn down the heat and add whole peaches. Simmer for about 5–8 minutes, turning from time to time. Remove from heat as soon as peaches soften. Leave to stand in the fridge for at least 2 hours, turning from time to time.

Melon and Cucumber Salad

'Scotch' Eggs with Raw Fennel Salad and American Coleslaw*

Apricot Meringue Gâteau

Melon and Cucumber Salad

½ honeydew melon
7.5 cm [3 in] cucumber
3 sprigs mint
15 ml [1 tablespoon] yogurt
15 ml [1 tablespoon] mayonnaise
salt and pepper

Dice the melon and cucumber. Finely chop the mint and mix with yogurt and mayonnaise. Season to taste. Put in individual bowls and garnish with 2 or 3 mint leaves.

* See page 77.

'Scotch' Eggs

Hard-boil eggs and leave to cool. Make a panada with flour, butter and milk. Add buckwheat and continue cooking for 5 minutes. Add peanuts and seasoning and leave to cool. Divide peanut mixture into 4 and shape round each egg. Dip in beaten egg and breadcrumbs and deep fry.

4 large eggs
50 g [2 oz] buckwheat flour
100 g [4 oz] ground peanuts
50 g [2 oz] plain flour
50 g [2 oz] butter
300 ml [12 fl.oz] milk
salt and pepper
50 g [2 oz] dried bread crumbs
1 beaten egg

Raw Fennel Salad

Chop all ingredients finely and mix with herbs and pepper. Toss in dressing and serve at once.

1 medium fennel heart
8 radishes
4 spring onions
2 sticks celery
30 ml [2 tablespoons] oil and
    vinegar dressing
½ teaspoon marjoram
black pepper

Apricot Meringue Gâteau

Soak apricots in water overnight. Whisk egg whites very stiffly and then gradually whisk in half the sugar. Fold in the rest of the sugar with the nuts, bicarbonate of soda and vanilla essence. Spread the meringue into 2 thin equal-sized rounds on rice paper on a baking sheet. Bake in a low oven 130°C/250°F/Gas Mark ½ for about 2½ hours until dried out. Allow to cool on a wire rack. Drain apricots and simmer with honey and 125 ml [¼ pint] water for 30 minutes until soft. Purée and allow to cool. Whisk cream until thick. Place a layer of meringue on a serving dish and spread with apricot purée and then with cream. Top with the second layer of meringue and sprinkle with chopped nuts.

Meringue
2 egg whites
100 g [4 oz] caster sugar
50 g [2 oz] ground hazelnuts
pinch bicarbonate of soda
vanilla essence

Filling
100 g [4 oz] dried apricots
125 ml [¼ pint] water
1 tablespoon honey
125 ml [¼ pint] double cream

Avocado with Orange

Egg and Almond Salad with Cumin
Cabbage

Chocolate Truffle Pudding

Avocado with Orange

2 avocados
2 oranges
30 ml [2 tablespoons] mayonnaise
sprinkle of coriander
½ teaspoon marjoram
salt and pepper

Peel oranges and remove pith and centre core. Chop and mix with mayonnaise. Add marjoram, coriander and seasoning to taste. Halve and stone avocados and fill the centres with orange sauce. Serve remaining sauce in a bowl.

Egg and Almond Salad

6 hard-boiled eggs
2 tablespoons flaked almonds
150 g [2 oz] Cheshire cheese
4 beetroot
½ cucumber
4 spring onions
50 g [2 oz] mushrooms
4 tomatoes
chopped parsley
60 ml [4 tablespoons] mayonnaise
salt and pepper

Dice all ingredients except tomato and parsley and mix with the seasoning and mayonnaise. Heap onto a serving dish and surround with sliced tomato. Sprinkle with parsley.

Cumin Cabbage

½ medium hearted cabbage
½ bunch watercress
60 ml [4 tablespoons] oil and
   lemon dressing
¼ teaspoon ground cumin seed
salt and pepper

Mix cumin seed with oil and lemon dressing. Season to taste and pour over shredded cabbage and watercress.

Chocolate Truffle Pudding

Melt butter and honey or sugar in a pan. Do not allow to boil. Remove from heat and add cocoa, crumbs, nuts and raisins. Stir well and add chosen liquor. Press into a small tin about 10 cm [4 in] square and decorate with walnut halves. Place in fridge to set. Serve in small squares with freshly whipped cream.

150 g [6 oz] stale cake crumbs
50 g [2 oz] butter
50 g [2 oz] thick honey or
   Barbados sugar
1 tablespoon cocoa
1 tablespoon chopped walnuts
1 tablespoon raisins
15 ml [1 tablespoon] sherry, rum
   or brandy
4 walnut halves

Iced Cucumber Soup

Orange Banana Salad with Senegal Eggs* and Watercress, and Bean and Garlic Salad

Coffee Cheesecake Mousse

Iced Cucumber Soup

Melt butter in pan and fry chopped onions till golden. Add wine and bring to the boil. Add sliced potatoes, cucumber, vegetable stock and seasoning. Simmer for 30 minutes and allow to cool. Liquidize and correct seasoning. Serve chilled, garnished with fresh cream, chopped parsley and diced cucumber.

225 g [8 oz] potatoes
½ large cucumber
1 medium onion
50 g [1 oz] butter
125 ml [¼ pint] white wine
500 ml [1 pint] vegetable stock
salt and pepper
chopped parsley
2.5 cm [1 in] diced cucumber
60 ml [4 tablespoons] single
   cream

* See page 148, divide quantities by three.

Orange Banana Salad

2 tablespoons smooth peanut
  butter
1 teaspoon finely grated orange
  peel
25 g [1 oz] finely chopped
  crystallized ginger (optional)
2 bananas, split lengthwise
30 ml [2 tablespoons] mayonnaise
7·5 ml [½ tablespoon] orange
juice
50 g [2 oz] chopped peanuts,
  fresh or roasted
lettuce leaves

Mix the peanut butter, orange peel and ginger if used. Spread this mixture onto one half of each banana then top with remaining halves. Cut each into four. Mix mayonnaise with orange juice. Dip filled banana pieces into this and roll in chopped peanuts till coated. Serve on lettuce leaves.

Bean and Garlic Salad

100 g [4 oz] haricot beans
½ onion
1 stick celery
1 large pickled gherkin/cucumber
3 tablespoons parsley
30 ml [2 tablespoons] oil and
  vinegar dressing
7·5 ml [½ tablespoon] Worcestershire sauce
1 clove garlic
watercress
salt and pepper

Cook beans (see Chapter 4). Finely chop onion, celery, pickled cucumber, garlic and parsley. Mix with beans. Mix dressing with Worcestershire sauce. Pour over the bean mixture and season to taste. Serve garnished with watercress.

Coffee Cheesecake Mousse

Base
9 Digestive biscuits
40 g [1½ oz] butter
25 g [1 oz] sugar

Filling
225 g [8 oz] cream cheese
2 tablespoons honey
125 ml [¼ pint] natural yogurt
1 tablespoon instant coffee
65 ml [2½ fl.oz] water
12½ g [½ oz] gelatine or 2
  teaspoons gelozone
2 eggs

Crush digestive biscuits and mix with sugar and melted butter. Press into a 17.5 cm [7 in] cake tin and place in a low oven 140°C/275°F/Gas Mark 1 for 8–10 minutes. Allow to cool. Mix honey and cream cheese until smooth and gradually add egg yolks and yogurt. Boil water and mix with coffee and gelatine or gelozone. Allow to cool and mix with cream cheese and eggs. Whisk egg whites until stiff and fold into the cream cheese mixture. Pour on top of base and chill until firm.

Iced Cucumber Soup (page 63)

French Tomato Salad

Stuffed Eggs with Mixed Bean Salad, Carrot and Orange Salad and Potato Salad*

Blackcurrant Ice Cream

French Tomato Salad

Peel and slice tomatoes and arrange on four plates. Finely slice onion and lay on top of the tomatoes. Sprinkle with chervil. Mix all remaining ingredients to make a dressing and pour over the salad. Serve slightly chilled.

4 large Mediterranean tomatoes
1 onion
chervil
90 ml [6 tablespoons] olive oil
45 ml [3 tablespoons] wine
   vinegar
½ teaspoon French mustard
½ teaspoon sugar
salt and pepper

Stuffed Eggs

Halve eggs and remove yolks. Mix with the chosen stuffing ingredients and pile back into the egg whites. Sprinkle with paprika or chopped parsley to garnish.

4 hard-boiled eggs

Stuffing 1
10 ml [2 teaspoons] mayonnaise
2 teaspoons chutney
salt and pepper

or

Stuffing 2
20 ml [4 teaspoons] mayonnaise
½ teaspoon cumin or curry
   powder
salt and pepper

or

Stuffing 3
15 ml [3 teaspoons] mayonnaise
4 teaspoons grated blue cheese
salt and pepper

or

Stuffing 4
20 ml [4 teaspoons] mayonnaise
1 teaspoon ground walnuts
1 teaspoon marjoram

* See page 75.

Spinach Ravioli (page 50)

Mixed Bean Salad

25 g [1 oz] haricot beans
25 g [1 oz] black eye beans
25 g [1 oz] soya beans
25 g [1 oz] red beans
4 spring onions
60 ml [4 tablespoons] oil and
   vinegar dressing
black pepper

Cook beans as directed in Chapter 4. Finely chop spring onions and mix with beans. Pour over the dressing and season to taste.

Carrot and Orange Salad

2 large carrots
2 oranges
4 black olives
black pepper

Peel and coarsely grate carrots. Peel and chop one orange and squeeze the other. Add chopped orange and juice to the carrot and mix well. Use plenty of black pepper to season. Decorate with olives.

Blackcurrant Ice Cream

250 ml [½ pint] double cream
250 ml [½ pint] blackcurrant
   purée
2 tablespoons Barbados sugar or
   honey

Make the purée by simmering fruit in a little water and liquidizing. Mix in the sugar or honey. Whip cream until stiff and fold into the fruit mixture. Spoon into a container, cover and freeze.

African Fruit Salad

Napoleon Rice Cake with Indian Onion Salad and Cabbage and Pineapple Salad

Aduki Pie

African Fruit Salad

4 large Cos lettuce leaves
2 oranges
2 grapefruit
50 g [2 oz] roast peanuts
60 ml [4 tablespoons] oil and
   vinegar dressing
mint

Place one large lettuce leaf on each dish and fill with peeled and chopped orange and grapefruit. Sprinkle with peanuts and chopped mint and add a tablespoon of dressing to each dish.

Napoleon Rice Cake

Cook rice and peas, separately, in boiling salted water until tender. Drain and allow to cool. Chop nuts and onion and mix with rice and peas. Add herbs, dressing and seasoning. Press into a greased pudding basin and chill for 1 hour. Carefully turn out onto serving dish and reshape if necessary. Garnish with sliced beetroot just before serving.

150 g [6 oz] rice
150 g [6 oz] fresh or frozen peas
75 g [3 oz] walnuts
75 g [3 oz] almonds
1 onion
1 teaspoon thyme
salt and pepper
15 ml [1 tablespoon] oil and vinegar dressing
2 cooked beetroot

Indian Onion Salad

Slice onions finely and fry in a mixture of butter and cooking oil with curry powder. When soft drain off excess oil and add remaining ingredients. Continue cooking for 5 minutes stirring all the time. Allow to cool and serve chilled.

450 g [1 lb] large onions
25 g [1 oz] raisins
1 tablespoon Barbados sugar
30 ml [2 tablespoons] vinegar
1 teaspoon curry powder
butter and cooking oil

Cabbage and Pineapple Salad

Finely shred cabbage. Drain pineapple and mix with cabbage. Add lemon juice and sage and mix well.

1 small or ½ large green hearted cabbage
1 small tin crushed pineapple
juice of 1 lemon
1 sprig fresh or ¼ teaspoon dried sage

Aduki Pie

Rub fat into flour and salt and bind with water. Roll out thinly and line a 17.5 cm [7 in] flan tin. Place beans and raisins in base of flan. Cover with peeled, sliced apples. Pour over lemon and honey and sprinkle with cinnamon. Brush with apricot jam. Bake at 200°C/400°F/Gas Mark 6 for 45–50 minutes.

Pastry
100 g [4 oz] plain flour
50 g [2 oz] margarine or butter
pinch salt
water

Filling
75 g [3 oz] cooked Aduki beans
50 g [2 oz] raisins
450 g [1 lb] cooking apples
juice of 1 lemon
2 tablespoons honey
cinnamon
apricot jam

Courgettes Vinaigrette

Tomato and Oregano Cheesecake with Savoury Rice* and Waldorf Salad

Fresh Orange Compôte

Courgettes Vinaigrette

4 large or 8 small courgettes
1 large onion
90 ml [6 tablespoons] oil
45 ml [3 tablespoons] wine
    vinegar
½ teaspoon sugar
1 tablespoon chopped parsley
½ teaspoon French mustard
salt and black pepper

Wash courgettes and slice large ones in half lengthways. Cut into 2.5 cm [1 in] lengths and steam in a very little salted water for about 5–8 minutes until just tender. Drain and allow to cool. Finely slice onion and arrange with courgettes in small individual bowls. Mix oil, vinegar, French mustard and sugar and pour over the courgettes. Sprinkle with black pepper and parsley. Chill for 30 minutes before serving.

Tomato and Oregano Cheesecake

Base
10 unsweetened wheatmeal
    biscuits
40 g [1½ oz] butter

Filling
225 g [8 oz] cottage cheese
1 tin tomatoes
12½ g [½ oz] packet gelatine or 2
    teaspoons gelozone
1 teaspoon oregano
water
salt and pepper

Crush biscuits and mix with melted butter. Press into 17.5 cm [7 in] cake tin and bake at 140°C/275°F/Gas Mark 1 for 8 minutes. Remove and allow to cool. Place cottage cheese and contents of a tin of tomatoes in a liquidizer and blend. Prepare gelatine or gelozone as suggested in Chapter 4 and add to cheese and tomato mixture. Add oregano and seasoning and pour over the cold biscuit base. Refrigerate till set. Remove from cake tin and serve.

Waldorf Salad

2 eating apples
4 sticks celery
8 half walnuts
15 ml [1 tablespoon] mayonnaise
black pepper

Dice apples, celery and walnuts. Mix together with mayonnaise and black pepper.

* See page 76.

Fresh Orange Compôte

Peel and slice four of the oranges and arrange in a bowl. Grate a little of the rind of the remaining oranges over the slices. Squeeze the juice and pour over the rest of the fruit. Pour over the Cointreau and chill. For those with a very sweet tooth add 1 tablespoon of honey to the orange juice before pouring over the fruit.

5 oranges
1 miniature bottle Cointreau
1 tablespoon honey (optional)

Mushrooms in Red Wine

Pasta Nut Salad with Asparagus and Soya Bean Salad and Endive with Rosemary

Assorted Fresh Fruit Bowl

Mushrooms in Red Wine

Finely slice onions and fry in cooking oil until transparent. Add mushrooms and sauté for a further 2–3 minutes. Add all remaining ingredients and bring to the boil. Simmer for 30 minutes and allow to cool. Chill before serving sprinkled with freshly chopped parsley.

225 g [8 oz] button mushrooms
2 onions
300 ml [12 fl.oz] red wine
$\frac{1}{4}$ teaspoon thyme
$\frac{1}{4}$ teaspoon garlic salt
$\frac{1}{2}$ teaspoon fennel seed
2 teaspoons tomato purée
salt and pepper
parsley

Pasta Nut Salad

Cook pasta in boiling salted water until tender. Drain and allow to cool. Finely chop onions and green pepper and mix with pasta. Add nuts and raisins, yogurt and lemon juice and mix well. Garnish with a few more flaked almonds and raisins.

100 g [4 oz] pasta shells
50 g [2 oz] roasted peanuts
50 g [2 oz] flaked almonds
50 g [2 oz] raisins
1 green pepper
1 shallot or 3 spring onions
1 small carton natural yogurt
15 ml [1 tablespoon] lemon juice

Asparagus and Soya Bean Salad

150 g [6 oz] cooked soya beans
75 g [3 oz] tin of asparagus
2 sticks of celery
1 teaspoon basil
2 gherkins
black pepper
30 ml [2 tablespoons] oil and
    vinegar dressing

Drain asparagus and chop. Mix with soya beans and add very finely chopped celery and gherkin. Sprinkle with basil and black pepper and toss in oil and vinegar dressing.

Endive with Rosemary

$\frac{1}{2}$ large head curly endive
2 teaspoons ground rosemary
45 ml [3 tablespoons] oil and
    vinegar dressing
black pepper

Wash curly endive and tear into pieces. Mix rosemary with dressing and toss the endive in the mixture. Sprinkle with black pepper.

Iced Beetroot Soup

Peanut and Garlic Pâté with French Bread and Beanshoot and Onion Salad

Pears in Orange Juice with Baked Egg Custard

Iced Beetroot Soup

450 g [1 lb] cooked beetroot
125 ml [$\frac{1}{4}$ pint] vegetable stock
$\frac{1}{2}$ teaspoon Marmite or yeast
    extract
1 small carton yogurt
$\frac{1}{2}$ small carton double cream
juice of 1 orange
salt and pepper
2 sprigs mint
6 ice cubes

Heat stock and dissolve Marmite in it. Allow to cool. Blend beetroot, stock and yogurt in a blender. Add cream and season. Serve chilled with a little fresh orange juice poured in just before serving. Add six ice cubes and two sprigs of mint.

Peanut and Garlic Pâté

Mix all ingredients together until smooth and season to taste. Serve chilled in individual dishes with crusty French bread.

3 tablespoons peanut butter
100 g [4 oz] cream cheese
2 finely chopped cloves garlic
30 ml [2 tablespoons] single cream
few drops Worcestershire or Tabasco sauce
salt and pepper

Beanshoot and Onion Salad

Wash spring onions and slice lengthways. Finely slice green pepper and mix with onions and beanshoots. Toss in dressing and sprinkle with black pepper.

350 g [12 oz] beanshoots
1 bunch spring onions
½ green pepper
45 ml [3 tablespoons] oil and vinegar dressing
black pepper

Pears in Orange Juice

Squeeze oranges and mix honey with the juice. Peel, halve and core the pears and pour over the orange juice. Chill and just before serving sprinkle with chopped nuts.

2 large ripe pears
2 oranges
1 tablespoon chopped nuts
1 teaspoon honey (optional)

Baked Egg Custard

Beat eggs with honey and add warmed milk. Pour into a greased pie dish. Stand the pie dish in a tray of warm water and bake slowly at 170°C/325°F/Gas Mark 3 until the custard is set in the centre. This will take about 1 hour. Leave to cool.

500 ml [1 pint] milk
2 eggs
25 g [1 oz] honey
nutmeg

Artichokes with Renaissance Sauce

Rocky Mountain Salad with Orange and Watercress Salad

Stuffed Apricots

Artichokes with Renaissance Sauce

4 artichokes
lemon juice
salt

Sauce
250 ml [½ pint] natural yogurt
1 tablespoon tomato paste
1 small chopped onion
1 teaspoon dill seed
salt and pepper
paprika pepper

Boil the artichokes in salted water with a little lemon juice for 45 minutes. The leaves should come away easily when the artichokes are cooked. Remove centre leaves and choke and allow to cool. Mix all ingredients of sauce together and spoon into the centre of each artichoke. Sprinkle with paprika pepper just before serving.

Rocky Mountain Salad

Centre
150 g [6 oz] rice
3 eggs
1 small green pepper
3 large gherkins
15 ml [1 tablespoon] mayonnaise
1 teaspoon rosemary
salt and pepper

Surround
225 g [8 oz] cooked red kidney
    beans
100 g [4 oz] cooked broad beans
50 g [2 oz] cooked haricot or
    black eye beans
1 small onion
1 tablespoon chopped parsley
60 ml [4 tablespoons] oil and
    vinegar dressing

Cook rice in boiling salted water. Drain and leave to cool. Hard boil eggs and chop finely. Mix rice and eggs and add finely chopped gherkins and green pepper. Mix with mayonnaise, rosemary and seasoning and pack into a greased pudding basin. Chill for 1 hour. Mix beans together and add finely chopped onion and parsley and toss in dressing. Turn out the rice mixture onto a serving dish and surround with bean salad.

Orange and Watercress Salad

Wash and chop watercress. Peel and slice oranges retaining any juice that runs out. Mix watercress and sprinkle with black pepper and olives.

1 bunch watercress
2 oranges
8 black olives
black pepper

Stuffed Apricots

Simmer apricots in wine and honey for about 15–20 minutes until soft. Allow to cool. Mix cream, sugar, wine and brandy and whisk until fairly thick. Halve and stone apricots and place on a flat dish. Fill each half with brandy cream and add the juice to the base of the fruit.

8 apricots
125 ml [$\frac{1}{4}$ pint] white wine
1 teaspoon honey

Filling
125 ml [$\frac{1}{4}$ pint] double cream
40 g [$1\frac{1}{2}$ oz] Barbados sugar
50 ml [2 fl.oz] white wine
25 ml [1 fl.oz] brandy

Salad Medley

Potato Salad

Peel and boil potatoes in salted water until soft. Drain and chop. Add finely chopped onion and parsley and mix with mayonnaise and dressing while still hot. Leave to cool and season before serving.

450 g [1 lb] potatoes
1 small onion
parsley
15 ml [1 tablespoon] mayonnaise
30 ml [2 tablespoons] oil and
    vinegar dressing
salt and pepper

Red Cabbage and Walnut Salad

Very finely chop or grate cabbage and finely chop celery and walnuts. Mix with mayonnaise and season.

$\frac{1}{2}$ small red cabbage
2 sticks celery
25 g [1 oz] walnuts
15 ml [1 tablespoon] mayonnaise
salt and pepper

Savoury Rice

75 g [3 oz] rice
100 g [4 oz] mushrooms
225 g [8 oz] tin sweetcorn
½ green pepper
15 ml [1 tablespoon] oil
15 ml [1 tablespoon] vinegar
½ teaspoon thyme
½ teaspoon celery seed or salt
black pepper

Boil rice in salted water until just cooked. Wash in cold water and drain well. Finely chop mushrooms and green pepper and add to the rice with the sweetcorn. Mix oil, vinegar, thyme, celery seed or salt and black pepper and mix into the rice salad.

Winter Salad

100 g [4 oz] Cheddar cheese
2 large carrots
225 g [8 oz] sprouts
1 lemon
5 ml [1 teaspoon] olive oil
½ teaspoon cumin seed
beetroot, tomato or red pepper
   to garnish

Grate carrots and cheese and mix with finely chopped sprouts. Add oil, cumin seed, lemon juice and a little lemon rind and mix well. Pile into the centre of a serving dish and garnish with red vegetables round the outside.

Cheese and Beanshoot Salad

100 g [4 oz] beanshoots
100 g [4 oz] mushrooms
1 green pepper
100 g [4 oz] Caerphilly cheese
60 ml [4 tablespoons] oil and
   vinegar dressing
salt and pepper
sweet basil

Dice mushrooms, green pepper and cheese. Mix with beanshoots, herbs and seasoning. Toss in dressing and serve at once.

Sprout and Celery Salad

150 g [6 oz] sprouts
½ head celery
100 g [4 oz] mushrooms
3 tablespoons raisins
3 tablespoons cashew nuts
marjoram
60 ml [4 tablespoons] oil and
   vinegar dressing
salt and pepper

Finely chop sprouts, celery and mushrooms and mix with nuts and raisins. Add marjoram, seasoning and dressing.

American Coleslaw

Shred cabbage as finely as possible and add all other ingredients. Mix well and season. Add a little mustard if liked.

½ small white cabbage
1 small grated carrot
¼ small finely sliced green pepper
1 grated apple
1 tablespoon flaked almonds
1 tablespoon raisins
45 ml [3 tablespoons] mayonnaise
salt and pepper

Carrot, Raisin and Peanut Salad

Grate carrots and immediately mix with oil. Add all other ingredients and serve at once.

2 large carrots
1 tablespoon raisins
2 tablespoons roast peanuts
30 ml [2 tablespoons] oil
15 ml [1 tablespoon] lemon juice
black pepper
½ teaspoon dill weed

Beetroot Cream Salad

Cook beetroot and allow to cool. Dice and mix with diced gherkin and sour cream. Add basil and black pepper.

450 g [1 lb] beetroot
1 carton sour cream
1 large gherkin
¼ teaspoon basil
black pepper

Cucumber and Olive Salad

Coarsely dice cucumber and mix with finely chopped pepper and olives. Mix oregano and black pepper in the dressing and pour over the salad.

½ cucumber
8–12 black olives
¼ red pepper or pimento
30 ml [2 tablespoons] oil and
    vinegar dressing
½ teaspoon oregano
black pepper

Red and Green Pepper Salad

Finely slice pepper. Mix cream cheese and mayonnaise and season. Pour over the pepper and serve garnished with parsley.

1 green pepper
1 red pepper
50 g [2 oz] cream cheese
15 ml [1 tablespoon] mayonnaise
salt and pepper
parsley

7 Quick Meals and Snacks

This chapter includes twelve menus plus twelve quick snack recipes.

Melon and Mushroom Salad

Butter Bean Country Casserole with Spring Greens

Orange Syllabub

Melon and Mushroom Salad

½ melon
100 g [4 oz] button mushrooms
2 sticks celery
½ bunch watercress
30 ml [2 tablespoons] mayonnaise
salt and pepper
¼ teaspoon marjoram

Dice melon, mushrooms and celery and mix with mayonnaise, herbs and seasoning. Serve on a bed of chopped watercress.

Butter Bean Country Casserole

2 × 425 g [15 oz] tins butter beans
350 g [12 oz] mushrooms
4 small onions
6–8 tomatoes
100 g [4 oz] breadcrumbs
100 g [4 oz] cheese
cooking oil
salt and pepper

Finely slice onions and sauté until transparent. Add sliced mushrooms and continue frying for 5–6 minutes. Drain beans and chop tomatoes and add to the onions and mushrooms. Season and heat through. Place in ovenproof dish and sprinkle with grated cheese and breadcrumbs. Brown under the grill and serve at once.

Orange Syllabub

Grate orange rind into a measuring jug and then add juice. Make up to 150 ml [6 fl.oz] with liqueur. Leave to stand for an hour or so. Then add sugar and cream, whip to a thick creamy consistency. Serve with *petit fours* or sponge fingers.

1 orange
75 g [3 oz] Barbados sugar
250 ml [½ pint] double cream
Orange Curaçao or Cointreau

Peach and Chicory Salad

Chilli Bean Pie with Swiss Chard or Spinach

Fruit and Nut Case

Peach and Chicory Salad

Drain peaches and chop into cubes. Finely chop pepper and slice chicory. Mix with peaches. Add almonds and sweet basil. Mix oil and vinegar and add to the peach and chicory mixture with black pepper to taste. Mix well and serve slightly chilled.

1 small tin sliced peaches
3 heads of chicory
1 tablespoon flaked almonds
½ red pepper
1 teaspoon sweet basil
30 ml [2 tablespoons] oil
15 ml [1 tablespoon] vinegar
black pepper

Chilli Bean Pie

Slice courgettes and fry gently in cooking oil with oregano, black pepper and garlic salt. Cook peas in salted boiling water. Cook potatoes, drain and mash with butter and milk and black pepper. Drain courgettes and peas and mix with tin of beans. Heat through and spoon into an earthenware dish. Top with mashed potato. Fork and grill for 5 minutes until brown.

4 courgettes
100 g [4 oz] frozen peas
425 g [15 oz] tin 'Lazy A' red beans in chilli sauce
3 large potatoes
butter
milk
1 teaspoon oregano
½ teaspoon garlic salt
black pepper
cooking oil

Fruit and Nut Case

4 dried bananas
8 dates
4 dried prunes
8 dried apricots
1 tablespoon hazelnuts
1 tablespoon cashew nuts
1 tablespoon walnuts
100 g [4 oz] plain chocolate

Arrange dried fruit and nuts in an attractive pattern on a large serving dish. Break chocolate into pieces and scatter among the fruit.

Blue Cheese Dip with Toasted Rolls

Eggs Florentine

Orange Delight

Blue Cheese Dip with Toasted Rolls

4 wholemeal rolls (see page 49)
125 ml [¼ pint] sour cream
125 g [5 oz] blue cheese
75 g [3 oz] Cheddar cheese
½ small onion
black pepper

Finely grate cheese and onion and mix with sour cream. Season with black pepper. Place in a liquidizer for a few seconds. Halve rolls and toast under a really hot grill. Serve at once.

Eggs Florentine

450 g [1 lb] fresh or frozen
   spinach
4 eggs
25 g [1 oz] butter
25 g [1 oz] flour
250 ml [½ pint] milk
25 g [1 oz] breadcrumbs
nutmeg
salt and pepper

Cook spinach and drain thoroughly. Make a roux sauce with the butter, flour and milk, and season. Place spinach in a casserole dish and make four depressions in it. Break the eggs into these holes and cover with sauce. Sprinkle with nutmeg and breadcrumbs and bake for 10 minutes at 200°C /400°F/Gas Mark 6.

Orange Delight

Grate the rind of two oranges and mix with wheatgerm and then peel and segment them. Dip segments in yogurt and then roll in either wheatgerm and orange rind or in coconut. Arrange on a plate and serve with a few maraschino cherries for decoration.

4 oranges
2 tablespoons wheatgerm
2 tablespoons desiccated coconut
yogurt
Maraschino cherries

Piquant Onions
Pasta with Peanut Sauce and Garlic Bread
Brie and Celery

Piquant Onions

Peel and slice onions and fry in butter. Add all other ingredients and continue to cook for 15 minutes or until the onions are soft. Serve in individual ramekin dishes sprinkled with freshly chopped parsley.

450 g [1 lb] onions
25 g [1 oz] butter
1 teaspoon tomato paste
$\frac{1}{4}$ teaspoon chilli powder
5 ml [1 teaspoon] Worcestershire
   sauce
10 ml [2 teaspoons] vinegar
5 ml [1 teaspoon] soya sauce
salt and pepper
parsley

Pasta with Peanut Sauce

Cook pasta in boiling salted water. Finely grate onion and carrot and sauté in butter. Add peanut butter and stir in the milk and lemon juice. Add sufficient water to give a smooth creamy consistency. Bring to the boil and simmer for 5 minutes adding more water if necessary. Drain pasta and toss in butter. Serve with peanut sauce poured over the top.

450 g [1 lb] pasta

Sauce
1 small onion
1 carrot
2 tablespoons peanut butter
30 ml [2 tablespoons] lemon
   juice
125 ml [$\frac{1}{4}$ pint] milk
water
butter

Garlic Bread

1 small French loaf
2–3 cloves garlic
75 g [3 oz] butter

Finely chop garlic and mix with butter. Slice French loaf but do not cut completely through the base. Butter each slice and wrap in foil. Place in a very hot oven 240°C/475°F/ Gas Mark 9 for 5 minutes.

Breton Mushrooms

Cauliflower Macaroni with Green Salad

Honey and Ginger Yogurt

Breton Mushrooms

350 g [12 oz] mushrooms
50 g [2 oz] butter
2 cloves garlic
1 teaspoon thyme
salt and pepper

Finely chop garlic and fry in butter. Add finely sliced mushrooms. Sprinkle with thyme and seasoning. Fry mushrooms gently for about 5–8 minutes until soft. Serve at once.

Cauliflower Macaroni

small cauliflower

4 — 225 g [8 oz] macaroni
2 — 100 g [4 oz] cheese
1 — 50 g [2 oz] breadcrumbs
1 — 2 tomatoes
½ — 500 ml [1 pint] milk
25 g [1 oz] butter
25 g [1 oz] flour
salt and pepper

Cook macaroni and cauliflower, separately, in salted water. Make a roux sauce with the butter, flour and milk. Add most of the cheese and season. Place macaroni and cauliflower, broken into pieces, in a casserole dish and cover with sauce. Lay slices of tomato on top and sprinkle with remaining cheese and breadcrumbs. Place under the grill to brown.

or Cook in Oven at 190° for 10 mins

Hazelnut Terrine en Croûte (page 109) and Whitbourne Surprise Eggs (page 108)

Honey and Ginger Yogurt

Chop stem ginger. Mix yogurt with honey and ginger syrup. Add ground and stem ginger and chill while the rest of the meal is being prepared.

500 ml [1 pint] plain yogurt
2 tablespoons runny honey
$\frac{1}{4}$ teaspoon ground ginger
4 pieces stem ginger plus a little
  syrup

Dutch Beet Salad

Soufflé Omelette with Domodoa Sauce, New Potatoes and Spinach Mountain

Banana Nut Dessert

Dutch Beet Salad

Dice beetroot, cheese, cucumber and gherkin and toss in mayonnaise. Add coriander and seasoning. Serve on a bed of curly endive.

4 cooked beetroot
50 g [2 oz] Edam cheese
7.5 cm [3 in] cucumber
1 large gherkin
15 ml [1 tablespoon] mayonnaise
$\frac{1}{4}$ teaspoon coriander
salt and pepper
curly endive

Soufflé Omelette

Separate yolks from whites and mix yolks with milk and seasoning. Whip egg whites until really stiff and fold in the yolk mixture. Pour into a frying pan with hot fat ready and cook for about 3–4 minutes until the base is set. Finish off for another 3–4 minutes under the grill. Serve at once.

6 eggs
a little milk
salt and pepper

'Scotch' Eggs (page 61) and Rocky Mountain Salad (page 74)

Domodoa Sauce

30 ml [2 tablespoons] groundnut
  oil
1 finely chopped onion
½ grated apple
75 g [3 oz] ground salted peanuts
375 ml [¾ pint] apple juice
1 teaspoon turmeric
1 teaspoon salt
black pepper
30 ml [2 tablespoons] lemon
  juice
1 teaspoon sugar

Heat oil in a pan and fry onion in it with the turmeric until transparent. Add all remaining ingredients and bring to the boil. Simmer for 10 minutes.

Spinach Mountain

1 carton frozen spinach purée
2 teaspoons raisins
nutmeg
3–4 tablespoons double cream
salt and pepper

Stir spinach over a low heat until thawed and then continue cooking until all the liquid evaporates. Mix in the raisins, nutmeg and seasoning. Pile onto a plate and pour cream over the top. Serve at once.

Banana Nut Dessert

4 bananas
2 teaspoons flaked almonds
2 teaspoons chopped hazelnuts
2 small cartons plain yogurt
2 teaspoons honey

Slice bananas and arrange on a large plate. Mix yogurt with all other ingredients and pour over the bananas. Serve chilled.

Asparagus with Cumin Sauce

Sweetcorn Egg Nests with Almond Carrots

Fresh Fruit in Season

Asparagus with Cumin Sauce

450 g [1 lb] tinned asparagus
125 ml [¼ pint] sour cream
2 teaspoons ground cumin
salt and pepper

Drain asparagus and arrange on individual plates. Mix sour cream, cumin and seasoning and pour over the tips of the asparagus.

Sweetcorn Egg Nests

Parboil potatoes for 15 minutes. Peel and slice and lay in buttered individual ovenproof dishes. Sprinkle sweetcorn round edges to form a nest. Crack eggs into the centre and sprinkle with tarragon and seasoning. Dot with butter. Bake at 220°C/425°F/Gas Mark 7 for 15 minutes.
Note Use leftover potatoes for a really quick dish.

450 g [1 lb] potatoes
225 g [8 oz] sweetcorn
4 eggs
1 teaspoon tarragon
salt and pepper
butter

Almond Carrots

Grate carrots and cook in a little seasoned vegetable stock. When the carrots are cooked, drain and mix with almonds and basil. Dot with butter and serve.

450 g [1 lb] carrots
50 g [2 oz] flaked almonds
a little vegetable stock
$\frac{1}{4}$ teaspoon basil
salt and pepper
butter

Cauliflower Colette

Eggs Aurora with Steamed Vegetables

Eastern Apples

Cauliflower Colette

Separate cauliflower into florets and steam for 8 minutes. Drain and allow to cool. Mix curd cheese with rosemary and black pepper and shape into small balls. Arrange in a bowl with cauliflower florets and cover with sour cream mixed with lemon juice and salt.

1 small cauliflower
100 g [4 oz] curd cheese
30 ml [2 tablespoons] sour cream
10 ml [2 teaspoons] lemon juice
2 teaspoons rosemary
black pepper
salt

Eggs Aurora

8 eggs
2 onions
4 tomatoes
75 g [3 oz] breadcrumbs
4 tablespoons chopped parsley
cooking oil
salt and pepper

Hard boil eggs for 8–10 minutes. Meanwhile sauté finely chopped onions in a little cooking oil. As onions begin to brown add finely chopped tomato. Continue cooking for 5 minutes. Halve hard-boiled eggs and remove yolks. Mix breadcrumbs, parsley and egg yolks with tomato and onions. Pile mixture into egg whites covering the whole surface. Place under grill for 3–5 minutes to brown.

Eastern Apples

450 g [1 lb] cooking apples
6 chopped glacé cherries
1 tablespoon flaked almonds
1 tablespoon raisins
2 tablespoons honey
2 teaspoons candied peel
½ teaspoon cinnamon

Peel and slice cooking apples and simmer for 5–8 minutes in a little water. Mash with a fork and add all other ingredients. Serve topped with fresh cream.

Cheese and Semolina Soup

Sesame Potato Patties with Banana Sauce and Spinach

Fresh Apples and Dates

Cheese and Semolina Soup

2 tablespoons semolina
25 g [1 oz] butter
100 g [4 oz] cheese
1 litre [2 pints] milk
salt and pepper
nutmeg

Place semolina in a pan with butter and milk. Bring slowly to the boil stirring all the time. Add salt and pepper and continue cooking for 10 minutes. Add cheese and cook for a further 5 minutes. Sprinkle with nutmeg and serve at once.

Sesame Potato Patties

Boil potatoes until soft, drain and mash with butter. Add ground cooked soya beans, sesame seeds and seasoning. Mix well and shape into 4 large or 8 small patties. Coat with flour and fry in cooking oil until brown on both sides. Serve with banana sauce and spinach.

700 g [1½ lb] potatoes
350 g [12 oz] cooked soya beans
2 teaspoons toasted ground
   sesame seeds
50 g [2 oz] butter
salt and pepper
flour for coating

Banana Sauce

Mash bananas and mix with lemon juice and add a little water if necessary to give a creamy consistency. Finely chop onions and green pepper and fry in cooking oil. Add seasoning, herbs and banana mixture. Simmer for 20 minutes, liquidize and serve.

2 bananas
1 onion
1 small green pepper
juice of 1 lemon
2 tablespoons fresh mint
2 tablespoons fresh parsley
garlic salt and black pepper
cooking oil

Creole Nut Soup

Cheese Spaghetti Omelette with Watercress

Orange and Grape Salad

Creole Nut Soup

Sauté finely chopped onion and celery in butter until soft. Add tomato paste and flour and season. Blend in peanut butter and add milk gradually, stirring all the time. Bring to the boil and add tomato juice. Reheat and serve garnished with sprigs of watercress.

2 medium onions
4 sticks celery
3 tablespoons peanut butter
500 ml [1 pint] tomato juice
25 g [1 oz] butter
2 tablespoons flour
250 ml [½ pint] milk
2 teaspoons tomato purée
salt and pepper
watercress to garnish

Cheese Spaghetti Omelette

225 g [8 oz] spaghetti
1 onion
1 small green pepper
100 g [4 oz] mushrooms
2 eggs
100 g [4 oz] Cheddar cheese
salt and pepper
cooking oil
1 bunch watercress

Cook spaghetti in boiling salted water. Meanwhile finely chop vegetables and fry in cooking oil until soft. Add drained spaghetti and the well beaten eggs. Season and leave to set over a fairly low heat. Sprinkle with grated cheese after about 10–15 minutes and finish off under the grill. Serve with watercress.

Orange and Grape Salad

225 g [8 oz] seedless grapes
2 oranges
1 lemon
1 tablespoon honey
a few raisins

Peel and slice oranges and mix with grapes. Grate lemon rind and mix with juice and honey. Sprinkle oranges with a few raisins and pour over the lemon juice. Leave to chill while the rest of the meal is cooked and eaten.

Stuffed Artichoke Hearts

Mushroom Spaghetti Neapolitan

Cheese Board

Stuffed Artichoke Hearts

1 tin artichoke hearts
225 g [8 oz] frozen or fresh peas
125 ml [$\frac{1}{4}$ pint] oil and vinegar
　dressing
1 teaspoon tarragon
2 tomatoes
salt and pepper

Cook peas in boiling salted water. Drain and allow to cool. Arrange hearts on individual plates and stuff with peas, allowing them to overflow onto the plate. Garnish with tomato slices. Sprinkle with tarragon and pour 2 tablespoons of dressing over each serving.

Mushroom Spaghetti Neapolitan

Cook spaghetti in boiling salted water for about 15 minutes. Meanwhile fry mushrooms very gently in a little cooking oil. In another pan fry finely sliced onions until transparent. Add chopped tomatoes, tomato paste, herbs and seasoning. Cover with stock and simmer for 20 minutes until thick. Toss spaghetti in cream with mushrooms and serve topped with tomato sauce. Sprinkle with Parmesan to taste.

350 g [12 oz] spaghetti
225 g [8 oz] mushrooms
700 g [1½ lb] tomatoes
2 onions
250 ml [½ pint] water
1 tablespoon tomato paste
1 teaspoon oregano
garlic salt and black pepper
cooking oil
125 ml [¼ pint] double cream
Parmesan cheese

Jerusalem Artichoke Soup

Egg and Potato Tortilla with Buttered Green Beans

Fresh Fruit in Season

Jerusalem Artichoke Soup

Slice leeks and fry in a little cooking oil. Scrub artichokes and potato and remove any black bits. Slice and add to leeks. Cover with milk and stock and add herbs and seasoning. Bring to the boil and simmer for 20 minutes. Serve as it is or quickly pass through a mouli. Sprinkle with chopped parsley to garnish.

450 g [1 lb] Jerusalem artichokes
2 leeks
1 large potato
250 ml [½ pint] vegetable stock
250 ml [½ pint] milk
salt and pepper
cooking oil
1 bay leaf
¼ teaspoon marjoram
chopped parsley

Egg and Potato Tortilla

3 potatoes
1 onion
1 tomato
½ green pepper
2 courgettes if available
4 eggs
salt and pepper
cooking oil

Dice vegetables finely and fry gently in cooking oil for about 5 minutes. Beat eggs, season and pour over the vegetables. Turn the heat down low and leave to set for about 10 minutes. Turn over with a fish slice and cook for a further 10 minutes. Serve with buttered green beans.

Quick Snacks

Scramble Surprise

4 eggs
50 g [2 oz] ground peanuts
125 ml [¼ pint] water
½ teaspoon Marmite or yeast
   extract
salt and pepper
4 slices wholemeal bread
2 tomatoes
parsley

Place nuts in a pan with water and Marmite. Cook for 15 minutes until thick, stirring from time to time. Beat eggs with seasoning and add to nut mixture. Continue stirring over a medium heat until scrambled. Toast bread and serve scrambled eggs on the toast, topped with two slices of tomato and some fresh parsley.

Greek Salad

½ lettuce
4 tomatoes
10 cm [4 in] cucumber
12 black olives
watercress, radishes, spring
   onions in season
225 g [8 oz] Feta cheese
1 teaspoon thyme
½ teaspoon oregano
60 ml [4 tablespoons] olive oil
15–30 ml [1–2 tablespoons]
   vinegar
black pepper

Coarsely chop lettuce, tomatoes, cucumber and other salad in season. Arrange in bowls with the olives. Mix oil and vinegar with herbs and black pepper and pour over the salads. Flake the cheese on the top. Serve with hot Greek bread.

Welsh Rarebit on Toast

Make a thick roux sauce with butter, flour and beer. Add cheese and stir well. Next add mustard, Worcestershire Sauce and Cayenne pepper to taste. Toast and butter the bread and spread generously with the rarebit mixture and grill quickly until brown.

Note This mixture keeps for some considerable time in a covered container in the fridge.

4 large slices wholewheat bread
25 g [1 oz] butter
25 g [1 oz] flour
250 ml [½ pint] beer
100 g [4 oz] grated cheese
½–1 teaspoon mustard
Worcestershire sauce
Cayenne pepper

Nut Rarebit on Toast

Make a thickish roux sauce with the butter, flour, beer and milk. Add cheese and nuts and stir well. Add Worcestershire Sauce and Cayenne pepper to taste. Toast bread and butter. Spread the rarebit mixture generously over the toast and place under the grill until brown.

4 large slices wholewheat bread
25 g [1 oz] butter
25 g [1 oz] flour
125 ml [¼ pint] beer
125 ml [¼ pint] milk
50 g [2 oz] cheese
50 g [2 oz] ground roast nuts
    (peanuts, almonds, hazelnuts)
Worcestershire sauce
Cayenne pepper

Devilled Mushrooms on Toast

Gently fry whole mushrooms on both sides in butter. Toast bread and place one mushroom on each slice. Mix all other ingredients and spoon over the mushrooms. Quickly place under the grill and cook for 3–4 minutes.

225 g [8 oz] large field
    mushrooms (4)
4 slices wholewheat bread
30 ml [2 tablespoons] double
    cream
5 ml [1 teaspoon] Worcestershire
    sauce
5 ml [1 teaspoon] tomato
    ketchup
1 teaspoon French mustard
25 g [1 oz] butter
salt and pepper

Chilli Cheese Spread on Toast

1 small can beans in chilli sauce
100 g [4 oz] cheese
2 teaspoons marjoram
extra chilli powder as required
4 large slices wholewheat bread

Empty can of beans into a pan and mash with a fork. Heat through. Meanwhile toast and butter the bread. Remove bean mixture from the heat and add cheese and marjoram and more chilli powder if desired. Spread over the toast and place under the grill for 2–3 minutes.

Omelette Provençale

8 eggs
45 ml [3 tablespoons] milk
water
salt and pepper

Filling
2 onions
2 tomatoes
1 green pepper
1 clove garlic
1 teaspoon tomato paste
a little flour
salt and pepper
butter

Finely chop onion and garlic. Fry in butter until transparent. Add chopped tomatoes and peppers and tomato paste. Sprinkle with a little flour. Season and stir well. Allow to cook for about 15 minutes until the vegetables are tender. Beat eggs and milk and make either one large or four small omelettes. Fill with provençale vegetable mixture.

Crunchy Omelette Surprise

8 eggs
25 g [1 oz] flaked almonds
4 spring onions
milk
salt and pepper
cooking oil

Filling
225 g [8 oz] mushrooms
1 tablespoon cornflour
milk
salt and pepper
cooking oil

Finely chop mushrooms and sauté in cooking oil. When they are soft add cornflour and stir in sufficient milk to give a thick creamy consistency. Season and cook for 5 minutes. Beat eggs together and add flaked almonds, finely chopped spring onions and seasoning. Make an omelette with the egg mixture and fill with mushroom sauce.

Marmite Crumpets

Spread the underside of the crumpets with a little butter and place these on a baking sheet. Blend remaining butter with the Marmite and spread on top of the crumpets. Separate the yolk from the white, add the yolk to the grated cheese. Stiffly whisk the egg white and fold into the mixture with a little pepper. Divide between the crumpets. Cook in a moderate oven at 180°C/350°F/Gas Mark 4 for about 20 minutes.

4 crumpets
50 g [2 oz] butter
1 level teaspoon Marmite or
    yeast extract
50 g [2 oz] Cheddar cheese,
    grated
1 egg
pepper

Corn Potato Cake

Grate potatoes and finely chop onion and mix with sweetcorn, flour, eggs and seasoning. Fry in cooking oil on one side for 5–8 minutes. Turn over and fry on the other side. Serve garnished with watercress.

3 potatoes
2 onions
1 small 215 g [7½ oz] tin
    sweetcorn
2 tablespoons plain flour
2 eggs
salt and pepper
cooking oil
watercress

Cheese and Nut Patties

Cook potatoes and then peel and mash with cottage cheese and nuts. Finely chop chives and spring onions and add to the mixture. Season and roll in breadcrumbs. Fry on both sides in cooking oil.

700 g [1½ lb] potatoes
350 g [12 oz] cottage cheese
75 g [3 oz] ground peanuts
fresh chives or spring onions
salt and pepper
50 g [2 oz] toasted breadcrumbs
cooking oil

Devilled Beans on Toast

Finely slice onion and fry in a small pan in cooking oil. Add tomato paste, mustard, Worcestershire sauce, soya sauce and vinegar. Bring to the boil and add contents of tin of beans. Toast bread, butter and spread the beans on top.

425 g [15 oz] tin 'Lazy A' Boston
    baked beans
1 large onion
2 tablespoons tomato paste
45 ml [3 tablespoons] vinegar
30 ml [2 tablespoons] soya sauce
5 ml [1 teaspoon] Worcestershire
    sauce
1 teaspoon English mustard
cooking oil
salt and pepper
4 slices wholemeal bread

8 Breakfast and Brunches

Breakfast is perhaps the most important meal of the day yet it is sadly neglected by many people. Ideally it should contain some of all the essential nutrients and account for about 25% of all food taken during the day.

Breakfast is even more important for growing children so do make sure that they have something to eat before leaving for school. A glass of milk with the meal provides extra protein, as well as calcium and other nutrients. Fruit or orange juice at breakfast is also a good idea as it provides Vitamin C to help fight infection and to help in the assimilation of iron in cereals.

Good old fashioned porridge served with milk and honey is an excellent start to the day as it is a good source of both carbohydrates for energy and protein for body building. Muesli is another all-in-one dish that is popular at breakfast time. If you have a heavy day ahead, add a boiled egg and a slice of toast to the menu and you should have plenty of energy to last you until lunchtime.

Muesli was originally developed by Dr Bircher-Benner at his clinic in Switzerland to encourage the consumption of raw foods and particularly fruit. Nowadays there are many variations on the muesli theme, but in the original recipe the emphasis was on the fruit content rather than the cereals. Muesli doesn't take long to make. The cereals are soaked in water overnight and the fruit added just before serving.

With a little imagination you can easily make your own variations. Try mixing different whole grain cereals with the oats – some companies sell ready-mixed muesli bases containing four or five different grains. Use whatever fresh fruit is in season; blackcurrants, plums and mashed bananas are particularly good. Or use dried fruits in the winter.

Here is Dr Bircher-Benner's original recipe:

Apple Muesli

Mix lemon juice and condensed milk to a smooth cream. Add oats and stir thoroughly. Wash apples, wipe with a cloth and remove tops, stalks and any blemishes. Grate apple into oat mixture, stirring frequently to prevent discolouring. Sprinkle nuts over finished dish and serve at once.

4 level tablespoons rolled oats soaked for 12 hours in 180 ml [12 tablespoons] of water
60 ml [4 tablespoons] lemon juice
60 ml [4 tablespoons] sweetened condensed milk
4 large apples
4 tablespoons grated hazelnuts or almonds

Winter Muesli Mix with Yogurt

Mix muesli base with honey and yogurt and add raisins and walnuts. Grate pears, apples and a little orange rind into the mixture and stir well. Finally squeeze the orange and add to the muesli. Serve at once.

4 tablespoons mixed cereal base soaked overnight in 180 ml [12 tablespoons] water
1 tablespoon raisins
2 tablespoons chopped walnuts
2 pears
2 apples
1 orange
1 teaspoon honey
125 ml [$\frac{1}{4}$ pint] carton plain yogurt

Summer Fruit Muesli

Mix muesli base with cream and almonds. Finely chop melon and add to the muesli mixture. Serve sprinkled with fresh raspberries.

4 tablespoons mixed cereal base soaked overnight in 180 ml [12 tablespoons] water
2 tablespoons chopped almonds
60 ml [4 tablespoons] double cream
$\frac{1}{2}$ small melon
150 g [6 oz] fresh raspberries

Citrus Oats

4 tablespoons rolled oats soaked
    overnight in 180 ml [12
    tablespoons] water
2 grapefruit
2 oranges
125 ml [¼ pint] carton plain
    yogurt
1 teaspoon honey

Mix oats with yogurt and honey and grate a little orange rind into the mixture. Peel oranges and grapefruit and chop segments. Mix with oats and serve at once.

One of the reasons why so many people skip breakfast is that they believe it takes too long to get ready. But this doesn't have to be the case. Some of the preparation can be done the night before. For example, eggs for scrambling can be beaten up the night before and stored in a polythene container in the fridge; extra rice or potatoes can be cooked at dinner time and kept for the following morning; and pancakes can be mixed and even made the day before.

Extra protein is soon added to a standard orange juice, tea and toast breakfast by spreading the toast with peanut butter or cottage cheese, or grilling it with grated cheese and tomato.

Coddled eggs are quick and easy if you have some egg coddlers – they are made by most leading china manufacturers. Grease the coddlers well and break an egg into the bottom of each. Then add a knob of butter and any of the following flavourings: slices of tomato, finely chopped green pepper or mushrooms, mixed herbs, ground cumin or toasted sesame seed, or left over sauces. Screw down the lid and coddle eggs in a pan of boiling water for about 5–6 minutes until they are set. You can eat the eggs straight from the coddler or turn the eggs out onto buttered toast.

The Dutch have the quick nutritious breakfast down to a fine art and it might be worth taking a tip or two from them. They serve a variety of different kinds of bread – you could experiment with rye bread, granary bread, oat plait (see Chapter 9) or crisp breads of various kinds – with a selection of thinly sliced cheeses and hard boiled eggs.

Set out below are 8 really quick recipes followed by a selection of recipes for the weekend when you have more time or when breakfast becomes brunch.

Eggy Bread and Tomatoes

Beat the eggs with a fork and season. Cut the slices of bread in half. Dip them in the egg mixture and fry in hot butter. Slice the tomatoes in half and dot with butter. Place under a hot grill. Serve the tomato on slices of eggy bread.

4 large slices bread
2 eggs
salt and pepper
4 large tomatoes
butter

Indian Toast

Mix cheese, chutney and curry powder to a thick paste. Slice tomatoes. Grill bread on both sides and then cover with sliced tomatoes and then the cheese mixture. Place under the grill for 3–4 minutes until the cheese is bubbly.

4 large slices bread
2 tablespoons chutney
100 g [4 oz] grated cheese
4 tomatoes
1 teaspoon curry powder

Egg and Potato Pancake

Chop boiled eggs and mix with mashed potato and French mustard. Season and fry in melted butter until the underside is browned. Turn over with a fish slice and brown the second side.

450 g [1 lb] leftover mashed
  potato
4 hard boiled eggs
1 tablespoon French mustard
25 g [1 oz] butter
2 tablespoons chopped parsley
salt and pepper

Country Scramble

Finely chop mushrooms and tomatoes and mix with eggs. Heat milk and butter in a pan and add egg mixture. Season and scramble until cooked. Serve on toast.

6 eggs
50 g [2 oz] mushrooms
3 small tomatoes
25 g [1 oz] butter
90 ml [6 tablespoons] milk
salt and pepper
4 slices toast

Sunshine Crumpets

Poach eggs until set. Grill crumpets and spread with butter and tomato ketchup. Place an egg on top of each crumpet and season. Sprinkle with grated cheese and grill until the cheese melts.

4 crumpets
4 eggs
1 tablespoon tomato ketchup
100 g [4 oz] grated cheese
butter
salt and pepper

Stuffed Mushrooms

4 large field mushrooms

Stuffing
4 spring onions
2 slices bread
50 g [2 oz] cheese
2 teaspoons tomato paste
1 teaspoon honey
$\frac{1}{2}$ teaspoon marjoram
salt and pepper
stock
butter

Wash the mushrooms and quickly fry in butter. When they are partially cooked remove from frying pan and place in a heatproof dish. Make breadcrumbs from the bread and mix with finely chopped spring onions, cheese, tomato paste, honey, herbs and seasoning and moisten with stock. Pile on top of the mushrooms. Dot with butter and bake under the grill for about 5 minutes.

Bean and Potato Lyonnaise

350 g [12 oz] boiled potatoes
150 g [6 oz] cooked beans (soya, haricot or black eye)
1 large onion
1 tablespoon tomato paste
1 teaspoon marjoram
salt and pepper
a little water
cooking oil

Slice onion and fry in cooking oil until transparent. Slice potato and add to the onion. Fry for 5 minutes and add beans. Continue to fry gently until all ingredients are heated through. Sprinkle with marjoram and seasoning and add tomato paste mixed with a little water to give a creamy consistency. Toss vegetables in the tomato mixture until really hot. Serve at once.

Egg Bolognaise

1 large tin spaghetti in tomato sauce
4 eggs
50 g [2 oz] grated cheese

Empty the contents of the tin of spaghetti into a non-stick frying pan. Make four hollows in the spaghetti and break an egg into each hollow. Sprinkle grated cheese over the top and cook over a low heat until the eggs are set. Finish off under the grill.

Cheesy Rice with Mushrooms

225 g [8 oz] rice
100 g [4 oz] grated cheese
1 small onion
1 stick celery
$\frac{1}{4}$ teaspoon sage
salt and pepper
100 g [4 oz] button mushrooms
butter

Finely chop onion and celery and fry in a little butter. Cook rice in boiling salted water for about 15–20 minutes. When it's cooked, drain and mix in cheese and vegetables. Season to taste and add a little sage. Wash mushrooms and dot with butter. Grill until soft and serve with cheesy rice.

Brunch Rosti

Grate onions and potatoes and mix with beaten egg, Marmite and flour. Add seasoning and fry in hot cooking oil for 8–10 minutes. Turn over and cook the second side for a further 8–10 minutes. Serve garnished with sliced tomatoes.

700 g [1½ lb] potatoes
2 onions
2 eggs
1 teaspoon Marmite or yeast extract
1 tablespoon plain flour
salt and pepper
cooking oil
2 tomatoes

Savoury Mushroom Pancakes

Mix flour with egg and half the milk and beat well. Add remaining milk and seasoning. Leave to stand. Finely chop mushrooms and fry in butter for 6–8 minutes. Mix corn-flour with a little milk and then add remaining milk and seasoning. Pour over the mushrooms and bring to the boil stirring all the time. When the mixture has thickened simmer for a further 10 minutes. Make eight small pancakes with the pancake mixture and fill with mushroom filling.

Pancakes
75 g [3 oz] flour
175 ml [7 fl.oz] milk
1 egg
salt

Filling
225 g [8 oz] mushrooms
1 tablespoon cornflour
350 ml [15 fl.oz] milk
butter
salt and pepper

Apricot Brunch Bread

Soak apricots overnight, drain and chop. Soak All-Bran in milk. Cream butter and sugar and gradually beat in the eggs. Fold in flour and then stir in apricots, chopped hazelnuts and All-Bran. Place the mixture in a greased 450 g [1 lb] loaf tin and bake at 180°C/350°F/Gas Mark 4 for 1–1¼ hours. Turn out and serve warm or cold with butter.

100 g [4 oz] self-raising flour
25 g [1 oz] soya flour
50 g [2 oz] All-Bran
100 g [4 oz] butter
100 g [4 oz] soft brown sugar
50 g [2 oz] chopped hazelnuts
100 g [4 oz] dried apricots
125 ml [¼ pint] milk
2 eggs

African Kedgeree

225 g [8 oz] rice
4 hard–boiled eggs
50 g [2 oz] roast peanuts
1 teaspoon Marmite or yeast
    extract
½ teaspoon oregano
50 g [2 oz] butter
chopped parsley

Cook rice in boiling salted water and drain. Chop hard boiled eggs and mix with rice. Add oregano and peanuts. Melt butter in a pan with the Marmite. Add the rice mixture and toss over the heat with a fork until well heated through. Pile onto a serving dish and garnish with chopped parsley.

Lentil Risotto with Cheesy Tomatoes

150 g [6 oz] long grain rice
100 g [4 oz] lentils
2 onions
1 teaspoon ground cumin seed
625 ml [1¼ pints] vegetable stock
cooking oil
4 tomatoes
50 g [2 oz] grated cheese
salt and pepper

Finely slice onions and fry in cooking oil with cumin seed for 5 minutes. Add rice and lentils and fry for a further 2–3 minutes. Add stock and seasoning and bring to the boil. Simmer until all the liquid is taken up – about 35–40 minutes. Meanwhile halve tomatoes and pile up with cheese. Place under a hot grill until the cheese begins to brown. Serve with lentil risotto.

Buckwheat Pancakes

1 teaspoon sugar
half 12½ g [½ oz] packet dried
    yeast
250 ml [½ pint] warm water
100 g [4 oz] buckwheat flour
1 egg
salt and pepper
lemon juice and honey

Mix sugar and yeast with a little warm water and leave until it goes creamy. Add remaining warm water and whisk in the buckwheat flour. Leave to stand in a warm place until the mixture is full of bubbles. Whisk in a beaten egg and make eight small pancakes. Serve with lemon and honey.

Wholemeal Puffs

4 eggs
500 ml [1 pint] milk
5 tablespoons wholemeal flour
1 teaspoon salt

Separate eggs and beat yolks till really stiff and pale yellow in colour. Add milk and flour alternately, beating all the time. Add salt to egg whites and beat until really stiff. Fold egg whites into batter. Spoon into greased muffin or bun tins and bake at 230°C/450°F/Gas Mark 8 for 30 minutes.

9 Packed Lunches and Picnics

Too often packed lunches are regarded as just a stopgap between breakfast in the morning and a cooked meal in the evening. Yet many people, including growing children, have to eat them every day. Picnics, too, are often hastily thrown together without much thought for their food value.

There is in fact no real reason why packed lunches and picnics shouldn't be as healthy and appetizing as any other meal. The same guidelines apply and provided that at least one item is chosen from each of the four groups of food outlined in Chapter 3 the meal will be a nutritious one. Add some extra protein if the packed lunch is for growing children and cut down on the carbohydrates if it's for a sedentary office worker.

Very often the main problem with packed lunches is the time required to get it together. So if you are making packed lunches every day here are a few ideas to help cut down the preparation time in the morning.

1) Make salads the night before and keep in the fridge in airtight polythene containers. They will be just as crisp and crunchy at lunch time the following day. Do not add dressing to green salad or mushrooms, but add lemon juice and a very little oil to chopped or grated root vegetables.

2) Make double or treble batches of sandwich fillings and store in the fridge or freezer in airtight containers to use later in the week or month.

3) Make up batches of sandwiches and freeze in individual wrappings. If they are removed in the morning they will be thawed and fresh at lunch time. Avoid hard-boiled eggs or salad fillings if the sandwiches are going in the freezer. Also freeze pies and quiches in individual portions and you have an instant choice for lunch.

4) Keep margarine or delicatessen tubs and use to pack salad items, fruit salad or pâté. They are convenient and save a lot of mess.

5) Include fresh fruit, tomatoes, yogurt, cottage cheese or milk. They are all nutritious and require little or no preparation on your part.

6) Add a thermos of hot or cold soup depending on the season.

Keeping up the interest and variety is the second major problem for regular packed-lunch eaters. Sandwiches day in and day out can become extremely boring however exotic the fillings. So alternate sandwiches with homemade pies, pâté and rolls or quiche. Ring the changes on the accompanying salads and use different kinds of bread on the sandwich days.

Here are some ideas for different sandwich fillings and double decker sandwiches. Quantities vary depending on the number of people you are catering for and the size of their appetites. As a rough guide allow about 50 g [2 oz] cheese, 1 egg or 50 g [2 oz] pâté or spread together with salad items or garnish for a sandwich made from a standard size loaf. These ideas are followed by some recipes for picnics.

Sandwich fillings

Finely chopped hard-boiled eggs mixed with finely chopped onion, mint and a little mayonnaise

Grated Cheddar cheese mixed with grated carrot and black pepper

Ground roast peanuts mixed with mayonnaise and chopped watercress

Grated Cheshire cheese mixed with finely chopped celery, fennel seed and a little natural yogurt

Scrambled egg mixed with chopped chives and cumin seed

Peanut butter mixed with finely chopped shallots, fresh mixed herbs, a little honey and lemon juice

Cottage cheese mixed with chopped green pepper and flaked almonds

Finely chopped hard-boiled egg mixed with chopped walnuts, mayonnaise and cress

Cream cheese mixed with Marmite and watercress

Ground cooked soya beans mixed with Marmite, chopped tomatoes and herbs

Cream cheese mixed with chopped stuffed olives, gherkins and garlic salt

Mexican Double Decker

First layer
Scrambled egg and mixed herbs with sliced tomato
Second layer
Sliced cucumber, watercress, chopped green and red pepper and mayonnaise mixed with a little chilli powder

Cheese and Walnut Decker

First layer
Grated Cheddar cheese mixed with a little mayonnaise and chopped walnuts
Second layer
Watercress with chopped radishes and spring onions

Beet and Coleslaw Club

First layer
American coleslaw (see page 77)
Second layer
Sliced beetroot and grated Edam cheese

Nutty Parisian

First layer
Scramble Surprise (see page 92) and sliced tomatoes
Second layer
Lettuce, finely sliced raw onion and a thin slice of Cheddar cheese

Peanut Decker

First layer
Peanut butter and sliced pickled cucumber
Second layer
Sliced beetroot and watercress

Yorkshire Filler

First layer
Grated Wensleydale cheese
Second layer
Sliced apples, cucumber and mayonnaise

Barbecued Cheese Filling

75 g [3 oz] cream cheese
50 g [2 oz] butter
75 g [3 oz] red Leicester cheese
15 ml [1 tablespoon]
   Worcestershire sauce
1 teaspoon tomato paste
milk
salt and pepper

Blend all ingredients adding sufficient milk to give a creamy consistency. Place in the fridge and use any time during the following week. This quantity is sufficient for 4–6 sandwiches. Garnish with watercress, parsley or tomato slices.

Oriental Spread

150 g [6 oz] Cheddar cheese
2 bananas
8 dates
2 tablespoons chutney
salt and pepper

Grate cheese and mix with mashed bananas and chopped dates. Season and add chutney to give a smooth consistency. This quantity is sufficient for 4–6 sandwiches. Garnish with watercress, cress or cucumber slices.

Mexican Quiche

Pastry
100 g [4 oz] plain flour
50 g [2 oz] butter
salt
water

Filling
3 eggs
75 g [3 oz] cheese
1 small green pepper
1 small tin sweetcorn or
   Mexicorn
1 small onion
125 ml [$\frac{1}{4}$ pint] single cream
salt and pepper

Make pastry by rubbing fat into flour and salt and bind with water. Roll out and line a 20 cm [8 in] flan tin. Slice the onion and green pepper and simmer in a little water for 8–10 minutes. Drain well and mix with drained sweetcorn. Arrange in the base of the flan. Mix grated cheese with beaten eggs, cream and seasonings and pour over the vegetables. Bake at 200°C/400°F/Gas Mark 6 for 50 minutes to 1 hour until the quiche is set and lightly browned on the top.

Chestnut Picnic Pie

Rub fat into flour and salt and bind with beaten egg. Roll out and line a 20 cm [8 in] flan tin retaining sufficient pastry to make a lid. Boil potatoes and hard boil one of the eggs. Drain chestnuts. Slice cooked potatoes, hardboiled egg and chestnuts and arrange in layers on the pastry base. Beat the remaining two eggs with the cream and pour over the vegetables. Top with the pastry lid and bake at 200°C/400°F/Gas Mark 6 for 50 minutes to 1 hour.

Pastry
150 g [6 oz] plain flour
75 g [3 oz] butter
salt
beaten egg

Filling
225 g [8 oz] potatoes
3 eggs
285 g [10 oz] tin whole
    chestnuts
125 ml [¼ pint] single cream
1 teaspoon marjoram
salt and pepper

Leicestershire Picnic Roll

Chop Stilton and mix with walnuts and mayonnaise. Cut the French loaf in half lengthways taking care not to cut all the way through at the back of the loaf. Scoop out some of the dough from the centre and spread each half of the loaf with the Stilton mixture. Lay the watercress down the centre of the loaf. Close up the two halves and wrap in foil to keep fresh. Cut into eight chunks to serve.

225 g [8 oz] Stilton cheese
50 g [2 oz] chopped walnuts
30 ml [2 tablespoons]
    mayonnaise
1 bunch watercress
salt and pepper
35 cm [14 in] French loaf

Queensway Pasties

Finely chop mushrooms and fry in a little butter until soft. Drain well and mix with grated potatoes and finely chopped onions. Add beaten egg, flour, thyme and seasoning and mix well. Make pastry by rubbing fat into flour and salt and binding with beaten egg, retaining any unused egg to glaze the finished pasties. Roll out the pastry and cut into four oval shapes. Place a quarter of the filling in each one and join the pastry over the top, pinching it together between the finger and thumb. Glaze with beaten egg and place on a greased baking tray. Bake at 200°C/400°F/Gas Mark 6 for 30–35 minutes.

Pastry
150 g [6 oz] plain flour
75 g [3 oz] butter
salt
beaten egg

Filling
225 g [8 oz] mushrooms
2 potatoes
2 small onions
1 egg
1 tablespoon plain flour
1 teaspoon thyme
salt and pepper
butter

Whitbourne Surprise Eggs

4 eggs
1 teaspoon mayonnaise
½ teaspoon mixed herbs
500 ml [1 pint] water
1 teaspoon Marmite or yeast
    extract
3 teaspoons agar-agar
1 large gherkin

Hard boil eggs and allow to cool. Halve the eggs and remove the yolks. Mix the yolks with mayonnaise and herbs and stuff back into the egg whites. Push the two halves together to reform whole eggs. Dissolve the agar-agar in boiling water into which the Marmite has been mixed. Place the eggs in small moulds and surround with chopped gherkin. Pour on the agar-agar mixture and leave to set in a cool place.

Egg and Tomato Galantine

2 hard-boiled eggs
100 g [4 oz] rice
50 g [2 oz] breadcrumbs
2 sticks celery
2 onions
3 tomatoes
50 g [2 oz] ground almonds
2 tablespoons tomato paste
1 tablespoon soya flour
2 eggs
½ teaspoon rosemary
1 teaspoon oregano
salt and pepper
cooking oil

Cook rice in boiling salted water. Finely chop onion, celery and tomato and fry gently in cooking oil for five minutes. Drain cooked rice and mix with breadcrumbs and fried vegetables. Add ground almonds, soya flour, tomato paste and herbs. Season and bind with beaten eggs. Press half the mixture into a greased 450 g [1 lb] loaf tin and place the hard boiled eggs on the top. Cover with the remaining mixture and press down. Bake at 190°C/375°F/Gas Mark 5 for 1 hour. Allow to cool for five minutes and then turn out. Leave till really cold. Serve cut into slices with one of the picnic salads.

St Christopher Savoury Roll

Pastry
150 g [6 oz] plain flour
75 g [3 oz] butter
salt
water

Filling
150 g [6 oz] cheese
2 onions
2 tablespoons tomato paste
salt and pepper

Grate cheese and finely chop onions. Mix with tomato paste and seasoning. Rub fat into flour and salt to make the pastry and bind with water. Roll out and spread the cheese mixture all over the pastry leaving a small margin clear round the edges. Roll up the pastry and filling rather like a flattish Swiss roll. Place on a greased baking tray in a slightly curved shape. Cut across the roll leaving the pastry uncut at the side to make about 12 sections. Twist each section to lie on its side exposing the Swiss roll effect. Bake at 200°C/400°F/Gas Mark 6 for about 25–30 minutes.

Hazelnut Terrine en Croûte

Chop onions, celery and green pepper and mix with nuts, breadcrumbs, herbs and seasoning. Bind with beaten eggs. Make pastry by rubbing fat into flour and salt and binding with beaten egg. Retain remaining beaten egg to glaze the finished croûte. Roll out three-quarters of the pastry and place the terrine mixture down the centre of the pastry. Wrap the pastry round the mixture, sealing on the top and at each end. Roll out remaining pastry and cut out leaf shapes. Use a knife to mark out centre ribs and veins and arrange on top of the roll to mask the join. Press down with a little water on the joining surfaces and brush with beaten egg. Bake at 200°C/400°F/Gas Mark 6 for 45–50 minutes until the pastry is crisp and lightly browned. Allow to cool on a wire tray.

Pastry
225 g [8 oz] plain flour
75 g [3 oz] butter
2 eggs
salt

Filling
2 onions
½ green pepper
100 g [4 oz] breadcrumbs
75 g [3 oz] hazelnuts
3 sticks celery
2 eggs
1 teaspoon marjoram
½ teaspoon ground cumin seed
1 teaspoon freshly chopped sage
salt and pepper

Savoury French Roll

Cut French loaf in half lengthways but do not cut all the way through. Hollow out the centre and butter. Finely chop gherkins and chives or spring onions and mix with all other ingredients. Press into the centre of the loaf and close up. Wrap in foil or cling film and cut into 8 chunks for serving.

225 g [8 oz] cottage cheese
100 g [4 oz] ground cooked soya beans
3 pickled gherkins
15 ml [1 tablespoon] mayonnaise
1 teaspoon marjoram
1 bunch chives or 6 spring onions
salt and pepper
35 cm [14 in] French loaf

Date and Nut Quiche

Make pastry by rubbing fat into flour and salt and binding with water. Roll out and line a 20 cm [8 in] flan tin. Grate cheese and mix with beaten eggs, nuts, cream and seasoning. Stone and chop the dates and place in the base of the flan. Pour over the egg and cheese mixture and add a little milk if the mixture is not sufficient. Fork in, taking care not to pierce the pastry base. Bake at 200°C/400°F/Gas Mark 6 for about 50 minutes to 1 hour until the quiche is set and lightly browned on top.

Pastry
100 g [4 oz] plain flour
50 g [2 oz] butter
salt
water

Filling
3 eggs
100 g [4 oz] cheese
50 g [2 oz] mixed ground nuts
100 g [4 oz] dates
125 ml [¼ pint] single cream
milk
salt and pepper

Mixed Picnic Salad

1 small head fennel
2 carrots
¼ small cucumber
2 sticks celery
8 radishes
4 spring onions
juice of 1 lemon

Finely dice all vegetables and mix with lemon juice. If stored in an airtight polythene container the salad will keep in good condition overnight. Serve with fresh watercress and whole tomatoes.

Egg Waldorf Salad

4 hard-boiled eggs
2 eating apples
4 sticks celery
25 g [1 oz] chopped walnuts
10 ml [2 teaspoons] mayonnaise
salt and pepper
ground cumin seed

Chop eggs, apples and celery and mix with walnuts, mayonnaise, seasoning and a little ground cumin seed. Place in a polythene container and keep as cool as possible.

Beanshoot Salad

225 g [8 oz] beanshoots
1 pickled cucumber
2 carrots
1 tablespoon raisins
30 ml [2 tablespoons] oil and
   vinegar dressing

Shred carrots and mix with raisins and dressing. Cut cucumber into thin sticks and add to the carrots. Keep in the fridge until needed. Take the beanshoots separately and mix with carrots and cucumber mixture just before serving.

Celeriac Salad

1 large celeriac
60 ml [4 tablespoons]
   mayonnaise
salt and pepper

Peel celeriac and slice finely. Cut each slice into very thin sticks and mix with mayonnaise and seasoning. Leave to stand overnight in the fridge in a covered container. Serve at lunchtime the following day.

Buckwheat Cheese Biscuits

50 g [2 oz] buckwheat flour
50 g [2 oz] plain flour
50 g [2 oz] butter
50 g [2 oz] grated cheese
salt and pepper
water

Mix buckwheat and plain flour. Add salt and rub in the fat. Add grated cheese and bind with water. Roll out thinly and cut into rounds. Bake on a greased tray at 200°C/400°F/Gas Mark 6 for 15–20 minutes.

Oatmeal Picnic Bread

Mix yeast with a little of the warm water and leave to stand in a warm place for 5 minutes. Mix flour, oats and salt. Add oil, yeast, milk and water. Mix well and then knead for 5–8 minutes until the dough is smooth and elastic. Shape into a long roll and cut a pattern on the top with a sharp knife. Place on a greased baking tin and cover with a cloth. Leave to rise for an hour in a warm place. Then bake at 230°C/450°F/Gas Mark 8 for ½ hour.

50 g [2 oz] oatmeal
50 g [2 oz] rolled oats
350 g [12 oz] plain flour
12½ g [½ oz] dried yeast
125 ml [¼ pint] warm water
125 ml [¼ pint] warm milk
30 ml [2 tablespoons] salad oil
salt

Marmalade Fruit Loaf

Beat egg and mix with milk, oil, treacle, syrup and marmalade. Mix flour and raisins and add liquid mixture. The result should be a fairly stiff dough. Spoon into a well greased 450 g [1 lb] tin and bake at 180°C/350°F/Gas Mark 4 for 1 hour.

225 g [8 oz] self-raising flour
50 g [2 oz] raisins
1 tablespoon marmalade
1 tablespoon black treacle
1 tablespoon golden syrup
1 tablespoon corn oil
200 ml [4 fl.oz] milk
1 egg

Apple Turnovers

Rub fat into flour and salt to make pastry and bind with water. Roll out and cut into four oval shapes. Peel and slice the cooking apples and arrange half an apple on each oval. Add raisins and orange rind and sugar if desired. Fold the pastry over the apples and pinch at the side to seal. Place on a greased baking tray and bake at 200°C/400°F/Gas Mark 6 for 25–30 minutes.

Pastry
150 g [6 oz] plain flour
75 g [3 oz] butter
salt
water

Filling
2 cooking apples
2 tablespoons seedless raisins
orange rind
a little sugar (optional)

10 Dinner Parties Formal and Informal

Spinach Gnocchi

Ratatouille Roulade with New Potatoes and Broccoli

Apple, Date and Oatmeal Pie with Cream

Spinach Gnocchi

Gnocchi
225 g [8 oz] block frozen
    chopped spinach
40 g [$1\frac{1}{2}$ oz] semolina
25 g [1 oz] butter
375 ml [$\frac{3}{4}$ pint] milk and juice
    from spinach
salt

Sauce
25 g [1 oz] butter
25 g [1 oz] flour
375 ml [$\frac{3}{4}$ pint] milk
100 g [4 oz] cream cheese
2 tablespoons Parmesan cheese
salt and pepper
$\frac{1}{4}$ teaspoon celery seed or celery
    salt

Thaw spinach in a pan with a very little butter and cook for a few minutes. Drain and retain liquid. Make up to 375 ml [$\frac{3}{4}$ pint] with milk. Place in a pan with butter and semolina and bring to the boil stirring all the time. Add spinach and salt and continue cooking for 10–15 minutes. Stir from time to time. Pour into a bowl and allow to cool.

Meanwhile make a roux sauce with the butter, flour and milk and stir in the cream cheese and seasoning. Place two rounded tablespoons of the gnocchi mixture into small individual ovenproof dishes and cover with sauce. Sprinkle with Parmesan and brown in the oven for 15–20 minutes at 200°C/400°F/Gas Mark 6.

Ratatouille Roulade

Slice all vegetables and fry in a little cooking oil. Add tomato purée, wine, herbs and seasoning and bring to the boil. Sprinkle on the flour and stir. Simmer for about 1 hour until all the vegetables are soft and most of the liquid has been taken up. Line a 25 × 35 cm [10 × 14 in] Swiss roll tin with greaseproof paper. Oil the paper well. Make a thick roux with the butter, flour and milk. Separate eggs and add the yolks and seasoning to the roux. Next whip the egg whites until really stiff. Carefully fold into the sauce and pour into the lined tin. Cook at 200°C/400°F/Gas Mark 6 for 15 minutes. Remove from oven and pour two thirds of the ratatouille mixture over the Roulade. Roll up, removing the greaseproof paper as you go. Serve with remaining ratatouille on either side.

Roulade
5 eggs
$12\frac{1}{2}$ g [$\frac{1}{2}$ oz] butter
$12\frac{1}{2}$ g [$\frac{1}{2}$ oz] flour
125 ml [$\frac{1}{4}$ pint] milk
salt and pepper

Ratatouille Filling
225 g [8 oz] onions
225 g [8 oz] courgettes
225 g [8 oz] tomatoes
1 aubergine
1 green pepper
2 tablespoons tomato purée
125 ml [$\frac{1}{4}$ pint] white wine
$\frac{1}{2}$ tablespoon flour
$\frac{1}{2}$ teaspoon oregano
salt and pepper
cooking oil

Apple, Date and Oatmeal Pie

Rub margarine into oats and flour. When crumbly mix with sugar and bind with a little water. Divide into two and press half into a 20 cm [8 in] flan tin. Fill with cooking apples that have been stewed with a little lemon rind and juice. Arrange dates on the top. Roll out the second half of the pastry and place on top of the pie. The pastry is very crumbly and it may be necessary to do this in two halves joining the pastry with a little water across the centre. Bake for 1 hour at 200°C/400°F/Gas Mark 6. Serve hot or cold with fresh cream.

Pastry
100 g [4 oz] margarine
100 g [4 oz] porridge oats
100 g [4 oz] plain flour
100 g [4 oz] soft brown sugar
water to mix

Filling
450 g [1 lb] cooking apples
1 lemon
50 g [2 oz] stoned dates

Artichokes with Roquefort Dressing

Asparagus Delight with Baked Vegetable Rice and Lettuce with Minted Peas

Plum Cheesecake

Artichokes with Roquefort Dressing

4 artichokes
lemon juice
salt

Dressing
120 ml [8 tablespoons] salad oil
60 ml [4 tablespoons] vinegar
6 small gherkins
$\frac{1}{4}$ red pepper
75 g [3 oz] Roquefort cheese
salt and pepper
$\frac{1}{4}$ teaspoon sugar

Beat oil and vinegar together with a fork and add sugar and seasoning. Finely chop gherkin, red pepper and cheese and add to the dressing. Boil artichokes for 45 minutes in salted water with a dash of lemon juice. The artichokes are cooked when the leaves come away easily. Remove the centre leaves and the choke and fill with dressing. The artichokes can be served this way hot or cold.

Asparagus Delight

Pancakes
100 g [4 oz] flour
250 ml [$\frac{1}{2}$ pint] milk
2 eggs
salt

Fillings
40 g [$1\frac{1}{2}$ oz] flour
40 g [$1\frac{1}{2}$ oz] butter
milk
125 ml [$\frac{1}{4}$ pint] wine
225 g [8 oz] mushrooms
350 g [12 oz] can asparagus
cooking oil
salt and pepper

Mix flour, salt, egg yolks and milk. Whip egg white until really stiff and fold into the flour mixture. Use the batter to make 4 thick pancakes and keep warm. Finely chop mushrooms and fry in a little cooking oil. Make a roux sauce with the flour, butter and the liquid from the tin of asparagus made up to about 500 ml [1 pint] with milk. Add a little wine; season to taste. The sauce should be fairly thick. Divide into two and add the mushrooms to one half and the chopped asparagus to the other half. Lay one pancake on a serving dish and cover with half the mushroom sauce. Add another pancake and cover with half the asparagus sauce. Continue with alternate layers ending with asparagus. Decorate with parsley and serve at once. Cut like a cake.

Baked Vegetable Rice

Mix all ingredients and place in a casserole dish. Dot with butter and bake at 180°C/350°F/Gas Mark 4 for 1 hour.

50 g [2 oz] cooked rice
100 g [4 oz] cooked diced new
   potatoes
225 g [8 oz] diced marrow
50 g [2 oz] diced red pepper
25 g [1 oz] grated cheese
butter
salt and pepper

Lettuce with Minted Peas

Wash lettuces and slice into four quarters. Melt butter in a pan and turn down the heat as low as possible. Add quartered lettuces and peas. Sprinkle with chopped mint and seasoning. Cover with a lid and simmer for about 8 minutes.

For a change substitute finely chopped fried onion or $\frac{1}{4}$ teaspoon thyme for the mint.

hearts of 3 lettuces
700 g [1½ lb] thawed or fresh
   peas
6 teaspoons chopped fresh mint
75 g [3 oz] butter
salt and pepper

Plum Cheesecake

Make the base by melting the margarine and adding the crushed biscuits. Press into the base of a 22.5 cm [9 in] loose-bottomed cake tin. Stone the plums and place on top of the base. Cream margarine and honey until light and fluffy and gradually beat in the cream cheese, sour cream and egg yolks. Add a little lemon juice and some grated lemon rind. Whisk the egg whites until stiff and fold into the cream cheese mixture. Pour into the cake tin and bake for 1 hour at 180°C/350°F/Gas Mark 4 until set and turning golden brown. Reduce the oven to 150°C/300°F/Gas Mark 2. Beat together yogurt and honey with a little more lemon juice and pour over the top of the cheesecake. Smooth with a palate knife. Bake for a further 15 minutes until set.

Base
25 g [1 oz] margarine or butter
9 digestive biscuits
225 g [8 oz] fresh, stewed or
   tinned plums

Topping
50 g [2 oz] margarine
2 tablespoons runny honey
225 g [8 oz] Philadelphia cream
   cheese
125 ml [¼ pint] sour cream
2 eggs
1 lemon

Finish
125 ml [¼ pint] natural yogurt
1 tablespoon honey

Cauliflower Soufflé

Potato and Mushroom Céleste with Green Salad in Tarragon Dressing

Apricots Monte Carlo with Apricot Ice Cream

Cauliflower Soufflé

1 cauliflower
3 eggs
salt and pepper

Steam cauliflower until soft and rub through a sieve or mouli. Leave to cool. Separate eggs and mix yolks with cauliflower and salt and pepper. Whip egg whites until stiff and fold into the cauliflower mixture. Pour into four individual soufflé dishes and bake at 200°C/400°F/Gas Mark 6 for 10–15 minutes until set and slightly brown on top.

Potato and Mushroom Céleste

700 g [1½ lb] potatoes
3 onions
4 tomatoes
225 g [8 oz] mushrooms
225 g [8 oz] Brie cheese
1 teaspoon summer savory
½ teaspoon garlic salt
125 ml [¼ pint] double cream
salt and pepper

Peel and slice onions, potatoes and tomatoes. Slice mushrooms and cheese and layer all ingredients in a casserole dish. Sprinkle the layers with herbs and seasoning. Finish off with a layer of potatoes and pour the cream over the top. Cover and bake at 200°C/400°F/Gas Mark 6 for about ¾ hour.

Green Salad in Tarragon Dressing

Salad
1 lettuce
5 cm [2 in] cucumber
¼ green pepper
¼ bunch watercress

Dressing
60 ml [4 tablespoons] salad oil
30 ml [2 tablespoons] tarragon
   vinegar
¼ teaspoon sugar
1 teaspoon chopped fresh
   tarragon
salt and pepper

Wash lettuce and watercress and arrange in a bowl. Add sliced cucumber and green pepper. Mix dressing and pour over the salad.

Apricots Monte Carlo

Put 1 scoop of honey ice cream into each of four glass dishes and leave in the fridge. Drain the apricots well. Melt the butter in a flambé dish or frying pan and add the apricots. Thoroughly warm through. Sprinkle over the pine kernels and pour over the Cognac. Heat gently and set light to the Cognac. Add a little of the apricot mixture to each dish, top with apricot ice cream and serve decorated with the almonds, cherries and walnuts.

4 scoops honey ice cream
(see page 125)
4 scoops apricot ice cream
(see below)
large tin apricots
25 g [1 oz] butter
50 g [2 oz] pine kernels
3 liqueur glasses Cognac
12½ g [½ oz] almonds
12 red and green glacé cherries
4 walnuts

Apricot Ice Cream

Make purée by soaking 100 g [4 oz] apricots overnight, draining and simmering with 150 ml [6 fl.oz] water. Rub through sieve or mouli, mix in the sugar and allow to cool. Whip cream until stiff and fold in the fruit mixture. Spoon into a container, cover and freeze.

250 ml [½ pint] double cream
100 g [4 oz] dried apricots
2 tablespoons Barbados sugar or
honey
water

Egg and Tarragon Mousse

**French Onion Tart with Stuffed Potatoes
and Savoy Peas**

Orange Nut Crumble

Egg and Tarragon Mousse

Whip cream until fairly stiff. Sieve eggs, reserving 4 slices for garnish, and mix with cream. Prepare gelatine or gelozone as suggested in Chapter 4 and add to egg and cream mixture. Add remaining ingredients and mix well. Pour into individual ramekin dishes. Place a slice of egg on top of each and push into the mixture until it lies flat. Place in the fridge for at least 2 hours before serving. Garnish with a little more freshly chopped or dried tarragon. Serve with hot toast.

4 hard-boiled eggs
125 ml [¼ pint] double cream
45 ml [3 tablespoons] natural
yogurt
1 teaspoon tarragon
¼ teaspoon Worcestershire sauce
12½ g [½ oz] gelatine or 2
teaspoons gelozone
60 ml [4 tablespoons] water
salt and pepper

French Onion Tart

Pastry
75 g [3 oz] plain flour
25 g [1 oz] butter
1 egg yolk
salt

Filling
1¼ kg [2½ lb] onions
2 eggs
125 ml [¼ pint] double cream
50 g [2 oz] grated Gruyère
    cheese
1 teaspoon sugar
nutmeg
salt and pepper
cooking oil

Make pastry by rubbing fat into flour and salt and binding with egg yolk and a little water if necessary. Allow to rest and then roll out to line a 20 cm [8 in] flan case. Gently fry sliced onions in cooking oil and add sugar. When the onions turn golden in colour drain off any excess fat and mix in beaten eggs, cream, cheese and nutmeg. Season and spoon into the pastry case. Bake at 220°C/425°F/Gas Mark 7 for 40–45 minutes.

Stuffed Potatoes

4 potatoes
50 g [2 oz] butter
½ green pepper
1 tomato
salt and pepper

Scrub potatoes well and cut the skin all the way round each potato to prevent them bursting in the oven. Bake in a hot oven 220°C/425°F/Gas Mark 7 for 45 minutes–1 hour depending on size. Meanwhile skin tomato and chop finely. Fry with finely chopped green pepper in a little butter. When the pepper is soft allow mixture to cool. Mix into a paste with remaining butter and season to taste. When the potatoes are cooked, slit down the centre and again at right angles to the first cut and stuff each potato with a quarter of the pepper mixture.

Savoy Peas

225 g [8 oz] frozen or fresh peas
2 leeks
1 clove garlic
salt and pepper
vegetable stock

Wash and slice leeks and arrange in a casserole dish with the peas. Add crushed garlic, seasoning and enough vegetable stock to come about a third of the way up the vegetables. Bake on the lower shelf of the oven at 220°C/425°F/Gas Mark 7 for about 45 minutes.

Orange Nut Crumble

Gently stew fruit until soft and place in the base of greased pie dish. Rub fat into flour and nuts until crumbly. Add sugar and grated orange rind. Pour the juice of the orange over the fruit and then sprinkle the crumble over the top. Press down lightly. Bake in a moderate oven 190°C/375°F/ Gas Mark 5 for about half an hour. Serve with fresh cream.

Note This dish can be started at 220°C/425°F/Gas Mark 7 and then turned down after about 10–15 minutes.

450 g [1 lb] fruit (apples, plums or gooseberries)
50 g [2 oz] Barbados sugar or honey
a little water

Crumble Topping
75 g [3 oz] butter or margarine
100 g [4 oz] plain flour
75 g [3 oz] Barbados sugar
50 g [2 oz] ground nuts (almonds, peanuts or hazelnuts)
1 orange

Tomatoes Monte Carlo

Hot Cauliflower Mousse with Haricots Verts and Orange Beetroot

Potted Cheese with Oatmeal Biscuits

Tomatoes Monte Carlo

Slice off the tops of the tomatoes and put on one side. Scoop out the centres of the tomatoes and the seeds. Chop and mix with remaining ingredients adding sufficient cream or yogurt to moisten the mixture. Pile back into the tomatoes and cap with the sliced-off tops. Bake at 200°C/400°F/Gas Mark 6 for 20 minutes.

Note Any leftover risotto makes an excellent stuffing for baked tomatoes.

4 large Mediterranean tomatoes
75 g [3 oz] cooked rice
25 g [1 oz] cooked peas
a little sour cream or yogurt
$\frac{1}{2}$ teaspoon rosemary
salt and pepper

Hot Cauliflower Mousse

1 large cauliflower
2 eggs
25 g [1 oz] butter
25 g [1 oz] flour
50 ml [2 fl.oz] white wine or dry
    sherry
150 ml [6 fl.oz] vegetable stock
150 ml [6 fl.oz] milk
cinnamon
salt and pepper

Steam cauliflower and retain liquid to include in vegetable stock. Rub cauliflower through sieve or mouli. Make a thick roux sauce with the butter, flour and liquids. Add cinnamon and seasoning. Remove from heat and add beaten eggs and cauliflower. Pour into a greased soufflé dish and bake in a bain marie at 200°C/400°F/Gas Mark 6 for 1 hour.

Orange Beetroot

450 g [1 lb] cooked beetroot
15 ml [1 tablespoon] orange juice
rind of half an orange
butter
1 teaspoon sugar
black pepper

Dice beetroot and heat through in a little butter. Add grated orange rind and orange juice. Heat through again but do not boil. Sprinkle with sugar and black pepper and serve at once.

Potted Cheese

225 g [8 oz] Cheddar cheese
30 ml [2 tablespoons] port
$\frac{1}{2}$ teaspoon mixed herbs
$\frac{1}{4}$ teaspoon nutmeg
$\frac{1}{4}$ teaspoon English mustard

Grate cheese and mix with all other ingredients. Press into a small pot and leave in fridge for 3–4 days before serving with Oatmeal Biscuits. Serve at room temperature.

Oatmeal Biscuits

100 g [4 oz] plain flour
100 g [4 oz] fine oatmeal
1 level teaspoon salt
50 g [2 oz] white vegetable fat
25 g [1 oz] sugar
beaten egg

Sift the flour and salt into a bowl and rub in the fat. Add oatmeal and sugar and mix to a firm dough with beaten egg. Turn on to a floured board and roll out thinly. Cut into 10 cm [4 in] rounds and place on a greased baking tray. Bake at 170°C/325°F/Gas Mark 3 for about 15–20 minutes until pale brown and crisp. Cool on a wire tray.

Parmesan Eggs

Stuffed Avocados in Tomato Sauce with Cauliflower Almandine, Duchesse Potatoes and Minted Peas

Caribbean Ice Cream

Parmesan Eggs

Mix French mustard with a little milk and gradually add remaining milk. Beat in eggs with a fork and add marjoram, Parmesan and seasoning. Pour into individual ramekin dishes and place in a baking tin filled with 5 cm [2 in] water. Bake at 200°C/400°F/Gas Mark 6 for ¾ hour.

250 ml [½ pint] milk
4 eggs
1 teaspoon French mustard
½ teaspoon marjoram
2 tablespoons Parmesan cheese
salt and pepper

Stuffed Avocados in Tomato Sauce

Peel and chop tomatoes and place in a pan with water, tomato paste and seasoning. Bring to the boil and simmer for 15–20 minutes. Liquidize and keep on one side. Mix cream cheese with herbs and plenty of salt and pepper. Peel, halve and stone avocados and stuff the centres with cream cheese. Put halves back together and fix with a cocktail stick. Place in a casserole dish and cover with tomato sauce. Replace the lid and bake at 200°C/400°F/Gas Mark 6 for 20–30 minutes.

4 small avocados
100 g [4 oz] cream cheese
1 teaspoon basil
salt and pepper

Sauce
450 g [1 lb] tomatoes
2 tablespoons tomato paste
350 ml [12 fl.oz] water
salt and pepper

Cauliflower Almandine

Steam cauliflower until cooked and turn into a serving dish with the florets upwards. Make a thin roux sauce with the butter, flour and milk. Season and add almonds, retaining a few on one side. Pour over the cauliflower and sprinkle with toasted breadcrumbs and remaining flaked almonds.

1 cauliflower
12½ g [½ oz] butter
12½ g [½ oz] flour
200 ml [8 fl.oz] milk
25 g [1 oz] flaked almonds
25 g [1 oz] toasted breadcrumbs
salt and pepper

Duchesse Potatoes

450 g [1 lb] potatoes
2 eggs
25 g [1 oz] butter

Boil and mash potatoes and mix with butter and beaten eggs, retaining some of the egg to finish off the potatoes. Place potato mixture into a forcing bag with a no. 10 star nozzle and pipe into swirls on a greased baking sheet. Bake at 200°C/400°F/Gas Mark 6 until lightly browned (about 20–30 minutes). Brush the tops with the remaining egg when half done.

Caribbean Ice Cream

2 small pineapples
250 ml [½ pint] double cream
15 ml [1 tablespoon] dark rum
2 tablespoons Barbados sugar
glacé cherries
flaked almonds

Halve pineapples and scoop out the flesh leaving the skins intact. Refrigerate skins in a polythene bag. Purée pineapple with rum and mix with sugar. Whip cream and fold in the fruit mixture. Spoon into a container and freeze. Serve in the pineapple skins decorated with cherries and flaked almonds.

Green Beans with Peanut Dressing

Cottage Cheese Pancakes with Avocado Sauce, Buttered Vegetable Medley and Boiled Potatoes

Pineapple and Ginger Crush

Green Beans with Peanut Dressing

450 g [1 lb] French beans
2 teaspoons peanut butter
15 ml [1 tablespoon] milk
22 ml [1½ tablespoons] yogurt
½ teaspoon oregano

Cook French beans, drain and allow to cool. Mix peanut butter, yogurt and milk and add oregano. Place beans in individual dishes and pour the dressing over the top.

Cottage Cheese Pancakes with Avocado Sauce

Beat egg with a little milk and pour over sieved flour and salt. Mix to a stiff batter and beat well. Add remaining milk and leave to stand for 1 hour. Make eight pancakes with the mixture and spread each one with seasoned cottage cheese. Roll up and place in the base of an ovenproof dish. Make a roux sauce with the butter, flour and milk. Peel and stone avocados and sieve into sauce. Season to taste and pour over the pancakes. Place in a moderate oven 180°C/350°F/ Gas Mark 4 for ½ hour. Serve garnished with sprigs of watercress.

Pancakes
100 g [4 oz] flour
250 ml [½ pint] milk
1 egg
salt

Filling
450 g [1 lb] cottage cheese
salt and pepper

Sauce
50 g [2 oz] butter
50 g [2 oz] flour
500 ml [1 pint] milk
3 ripe avocados
salt and pepper

Garnish
sprigs of watercress

Buttered Vegetable Medley

Cook diced carrots or baby onions in boiling water for 10 minutes. Add remaining vegetables and cook for a further 5 minutes. Drain and add butter before serving.

100 g [4 oz] frozen or fresh peas
100 g [4 oz] frozen or tinned sweetcorn
100 g [4 oz] cut green beans
100 g [4 oz] diced carrots or baby onions
25 g [1 oz] butter

Pineapple and Ginger Crush

Finely chop stem ginger and mix with pineapple and yogurt. Chill before serving.

325 g [12 oz] crushed or chopped pineapple
1 small carton (150 ml [6 fl.oz]) plain yogurt
1–2 pieces stem ginger according to taste

Savoury Stuffed Apples

Spinach Lasagne with Tomato Sauce, Green Beans and Baked Fennel

Honey Ice Cream Cassata

Savoury Stuffed Apples

2 large cooking apples
50 g [2 oz] brown breadcrumbs
25 g [1 oz] ground peanuts
1 small onion
2 teaspoons toasted ground
   sesame seeds
2 teaspoons tomato purée
½ teaspoon oregano
125 ml [¼ pint] tomato juice
salt and pepper

Wash, halve and core apples. Slice each apple half into two layers. Finely chop onion and mix with all other ingredients. Place four slices of apple in the base of an ovenproof dish. Cover with half the stuffing. Place another layer of apple on top and finish off with the remaining stuffing. Bake uncovered in a fairly hot oven 200°C/400°F/Gas Mark 6 for 1 hour.

Spinach Lasagne with Tomato Sauce

8 pieces lasagne

Filling
350 g [12 oz] cottage cheese
1 kg [2 lb 2 oz] spinach
1 knob butter
1 teaspoon celery seed or celery
   salt

Sauce
450 g [1 lb] tomatoes
1 onion
2 tablespoons tomato purée
1 teaspoon oregano
salt and pepper
Parmesan cheese

Cook lasagne in boiling salted water and drain. Wash spinach and place in pan with a little butter. Cook gently until the spinach is soft. Spread each slice of lasagne with cottage cheese, spinach and celery seed. Roll up and place in a casserole dish. Make tomato sauce by frying finely chopped onions. Add chopped tomatoes, tomato purée, oregano and seasoning. Simmer until the vegetables are cooked through. Purée and pour over the lasagne. Sprinkle with a little Parmesan and bake 200°C/400°F/Gas Mark 6 for about 15 minutes.

Baked Fennel

2 large heads of fennel
3 or 4 shallots or spring onions
60 ml [4 tablespoons] vegetable
   stock
½ teaspoon Marmite or yeast
   extract
salt and pepper

Wash and roughly slice fennel. Place in a casserole dish and sprinkle with finely chopped shallots or spring onions. Mix Marmite with warm stock and pour over the top of the vegetables. Season to taste. Cover and bake in a fairly hot oven 200°C/400°F/Gas Mark 6 for about 1 hour.

Honey Ice Cream Cassata

Make ice cream by whisking eggs and honey until thick and pale in colour. Next whip cream and milk until really stiff. Quickly fold into the egg mixture and pour into a container and freeze. When the ice cream is frozen spoon a third into a small chilled metal mould and press down. Spread the remaining two thirds round the edge of the mould leaving a well in the centre. Whip cream and icing sugar to make the filling and fold in the chopped fruit and almonds. Spoon into the well in the centre of the ice cream, cover with cling film and return to freezer. Just before serving turn on to a serving dish and keep in the fridge until ready to place on the table.

Ice Cream
2 eggs
1 dessertspoon runny honey
75 ml [3 fl.oz] double cream
50 ml [2 fl.oz] milk

Filling
125 ml [¼ pint] double cream
1 tablespoon icing sugar
25 g [1 oz] glacé peel
25 g [1 oz] raisins
25 g [1 oz] glacé cherries
25 g [1 oz] flaked almonds

Stilton Pâté

Green Pepper and Hazelnut Bake with Tomato Sauce, Braised Endive and Parsley Buttered Potatoes

Lime and Ginger Syllabub

Stilton Pâté

Make a thick roux sauce with the butter, flour and milk. Cool thoroughly and add all other ingredients including finely chopped olives. Spoon into individual ramekin dishes and serve chilled with fingers of hot toast.

100 g [4 oz] grated Stilton cheese
5 ml [1 teaspoon] mayonnaise
25 g [1 oz] butter
25 g [1 oz] flour
200 ml [8 fl.oz] milk
1 clove garlic
salt and pepper
4 stuffed olives

Green Pepper and Hazelnut Bake

2 large onions
2 small green peppers
100 g [4 oz] mushrooms
100 g [4 oz] ground hazelnuts
100 g [4 oz] breadcrumbs
2 tablespoons soya flour
¼ teaspoon celery seed or celery
   salt
¼ teaspoon garlic salt
1 teaspoon fresh or dried mixed
   herbs
½ teaspoon summer savory
425 g [15 oz] can tomatoes
oat or millet flakes

Grate onions and green peppers and finely chop mushrooms. Mix all ingredients together and moisten with the puréed contents of the can of tomatoes. The mixture should be very moist. Shape into an oblong and roll in flaked oats or millet. Place on a greased baking tray and flatten slightly. Bake at 200°C/400°F/Gas Mark 6 for ¾ hour. Serve with tomato sauce.

Braised Endive

4 endive
1 small onion
¼ teaspoon Marmite or yeast
   extract
125 ml [¼ pint] vegetable stock
salt and pepper
cooking oil

Wash endive and place in a casserole dish. Fry onion until well browned in a little oil and add stock, Marmite and seasoning. Pour over the endive. Cover and bake at 200°C/400°F/Gas Mark 6 for ½ hour.

Note French endive is usually called chicory in Great Britain.

Lime and Ginger Syllabub

250 ml [½ pint] double cream
45 ml [3 tablespoons] ginger
   wine
15 ml [1 tablespoon] lime cordial
1 tablespoon runny honey
4–6 gingernut biscuits

Dissolve honey in ginger wine. Add lime cordial and cream and whip until thick. Chill and serve topped with crushed ginger biscuits.

Fennel and Avocado Salad

African Curried Vegetables with Dahl, Banana Sambal and Pilao Rice

Normandy Apple Tart

Fennel and Avocado Salad

Parboil fennel for about 5 minutes. Drain and slice. Finely slice red pepper and tomatoes and mix with fennel. Add herbs and dressing. Just before serving peel and slice avocado and mix in.

2 fennel heads
1 avocado
1 red pepper
2 tomatoes
½ teaspoon mixed herbs
60 ml [4 tablespoons] vinaigrette
  dressing

African Curried Vegetables

Fry onion in oil with spices until lightly browned. Add chopped vegetables and water. Bring to the boil and simmer for about 30–40 minutes. Drain liquid and mix with peanut butter. Return to pan and correct seasoning. Simmer for a further 5–10 minutes before serving.

1 onion
500 ml [1 pint] water
1 teaspoon curry powder
1 teaspoon cumin
1 teaspoon coriander
¼ teaspoon ground ginger
2 cloves
4 cardamoms
1 heaped tablespoon peanut
  butter
cooking oil
450 g [1 lb] mixed vegetables:
  cauliflower, carrots and
  potatoes
salt and pepper

Dahl

Place lentils in a pan with water and bring to the boil. Simmer for ¾ hour. Add turmeric and salt and continue cooking until lentils are really soft (about another 30 minutes). Fry sliced onion, garlic and ginger until lightly browned and add to the dahl just before serving.

100 g [4 oz] lentils
500 ml [1 pint] water
½ teaspoon turmeric
salt
1 small onion
1 clove garlic (optional)
1 piece stem ginger

Banana Sambal

Cook unpeeled banana in boiling water until soft. Remove from water and allow to cool. Peel, mash and mix with finely chopped onion and chilli. Add vinegar, yogurt and seasoning. Mix well.

1 banana
½ small onion
1 green chilli without the seeds
10 ml [2 teaspoons] cider
  vinegar
½ small carton natural yogurt
salt and pepper

Pilao Rice

150 g [6 oz] rice
1 onion
25 g [1 oz] butter
3 peppercorns
1 cardomom
1 clove
½ small carton yogurt
750 ml [1½ pints] water
salt

Fry onion in butter and add rice and spices. Continue cooking for 5 minutes. Add yogurt and water. Bring to the boil and simmer until all liquid is taken up (about 30–40 minutés). Correct seasoning and pile into a serving dish and if necessary dry off in a warm oven.

Normandy Apple Tart

Pastry
100 g [4 oz] plain flour
50 g [2 oz] butter
50 g [2 oz] sugar
beaten egg

Filling
450 g [1 lb] cooking apples
3 eating apples
apricot jam

Make pastry by rubbing fat into sugar and flour until the mixture resembles fine breadcrumbs. Bind with about half a beaten egg. Press into a 20 cm [8 in] flan tin. Peel and slice cooking apples and simmer with a very little water until soft. Allow to cool and spoon into the pastry case. Peel and slice eating apples and arrange on top of the apple purée. Brush with apricot jam. Bake at 220°C/425°F/Gas Mark 7 for about 45 minutes until the apples begin to brown.

Grape and Celery Salad

Courgette and Dill Soup

Avocado Risotto with Mexican Sauce and Red and Green Pepper Salad*

Hazelnut Soufflé

Grape and Celery Salad

225 g [8 oz] white grapes
7.5 cm [3 in] cucumber
4 sticks celery
¼ green pepper
30 ml [2 tablespoons] yogurt
¼ teaspoon rosemary

Halve and de-seed the grapes. Finely dice the celery, green pepper and cucumber and add to grapes. Mix all ingredients together with yogurt and serve slightly chilled.

* See page 77.

Courgette and Dill Soup

Melt butter in pan and add chopped onions. Sauté until transparent. Add sugar and sherry and bring to the boil. Add coarsely chopped courgettes, dill seed, vegetable stock and seasoning. Bring to the boil and simmer for 45 minutes. Rub through a sieve or mouli. Correct seasoning and reheat. Serve with a tablespoon of cream in each bowl.

450 g [1 lb] courgettes
1 medium onion
25 g [1 oz] butter
75 ml [3 fl.oz] cooking sherry
625 ml[1¼ pints] vegetable stock
1 teaspoon dill seed
½ teaspoon sugar
salt and pepper
60 ml [4 tablespoons] double cream

Avocado Risotto

Finely chop onion and fry in butter until transparent. Add rice and continue frying gently for 3–4 minutes. Add wine and bring to the boil. Continue cooking until all the wine is absorbed, stirring from time to time. Add herbs, seasoning, chopped avocado and vegetable stock. Continue cooking until the rice has absorbed all the stock (about 20–30 minutes). Add more stock if the rice shows signs of drying out too much.

350 g [12 oz] rice
2 avocados
1 large onion
50 g [2 oz] raisins
250 ml [½ pint] white wine
500 ml [1 pint] vegetable stock
50 g [2 oz] butter
½ teaspoon mixed herbs
salt and pepper

Mexican Sauce

Finely chop peppers and garlic and fry in cooking oil for five minutes. Add chopped tomatoes and all other ingredients and bring to the boil. Simmer for 20 minutes. Liquidize and correct seasoning. Reheat and serve with Risotto.

1 red pepper
1 green pepper
8 tomatoes
1 clove garlic
1 teaspoon coriander
2 cloves
½ teaspoon chilli powder
250 ml [½ pint] vegetable stock or water
cooking oil
salt and pepper

Hazelnut Soufflé

100 g [4 oz] shelled hazelnuts
125 ml [¼ pint] milk
25 g [1 oz] butter
pinch of salt
50 g [2 oz] sugar
60 g [2½ oz] plain flour
4 eggs, separated
butter to grease soufflé dish

Roast hazelnuts on an ungreased baking tin for 15 minutes at 200°C/400°F/Gas Mark 6. Remove from the oven and roll on a dry working surface so that the brown skin comes off. Grind the nuts finely. Heat the milk, butter, salt and sugar in a pan. Slowly add the flour. Stir until the mixture forms a smooth paste which comes away easily from the sides of the pan. Leave to cool. Beat together the egg yolks and grated hazelnuts and add to the sauce mixture. Whisk the egg whites until they form stiff peaks and fold into the mixture. Grease a soufflé dish and fill with the mixture. Place on the middle shelf of a pre-heated oven and bake at 180°C/350°F/Gas Mark 4 for 1 hour. Serve at once.

Hungarian Apple Soup

Cheese Fondue and Salads

Citrus Melon

Hungarian Apple Soup

4 eating apples
2 onions
1 red pepper
2 large gherkins or 1 pickled
   cucumber
1 clove garlic
500 ml [1 pint] vegetable stock
½ teaspoon sugar
½ teaspoon paprika
1 tablespoon chopped chives
100 ml [4 fl.oz] sour cream
50 g [2 oz] breadcrumbs
   (optional)
cooking oil

Gently fry chopped onions, garlic, eating apples, red pepper and gherkins in cooking oil. After 3–4 minutes add stock, seasoning and chives. Bring to the boil and simmer for 20 minutes. Stir in sour cream and serve sprinkled with more chives. For a slightly thicker soup add fresh bread-crumbs.

Cheese Fondue

Peel the garlic clove. Score one edge and rub over the fondue dish. Put in the water, butter, salt, pepper and nutmeg and bring to the boil. Chop the cheese into dice and add to the water. Leave for about 15 minutes to melt. If the mixture seems too thick add 1 tablespoon of water at a time until the consistency is right. Slice the bread. Light the fondue burner to keep the mixture warm, but not boiling. Each guest spears a piece of bread on a fondue fork and dips into the fondue. Serve with a medley of salads from Chapter 6.

600 g [1 lb 6 oz] Emmental
   cheese
1 clove garlic
grated nutmeg
125 ml [$\frac{1}{4}$ pint] hot water
25 g [1 oz] butter
salt and pepper
1 loaf French bread

Citrus Melon

Roast peanuts in the oven at 180°C/350°F/Gas Mark 4 for about 20 minutes. Halve the melon. Scoop out the seeds and flesh. Discard seeds and chop flesh. Mix with segmented and chopped grapefruit and oranges. Pile back into the two melon shells. Chop peanuts and mix with sugar and cinnamon and sprinkle over the fruit.

1 small honeydew melon
1 grapefruit
2 oranges
50 g [2 oz] peanuts
25 g [1 oz] sugar
$\frac{1}{4}$ teaspoon cinnamon

11 Gala Buffets

Recipes in this chapter are for twelve people

Love Apples

Hot Cauliflower Terrine with Spanish Lentils, Savoy Gratin and Chinese Cabbage with Juniper Berries

Lemon Tart

Love Apples

12 good sized tomatoes
125 ml [¼ pint] double cream
50 g [2 oz] grated cheese
sherry
salt and pepper

Peel and slice tomatoes. Place in individual ramekin dishes and cover with sherry and season. Place in a moderate oven 190°C/375°F/Gas Mark 5 for 20 minutes. Sprinkle with grated cheese and cream and continue cooking for 4–5 minutes. Serve at once.

Hot Cauliflower Terrine

2 cauliflowers
2 onions
150 g [6 oz] fresh breadcrumbs
250 ml [1½ pints] sour cream
4 eggs
nutmeg
salt and pepper
fresh parsley
butter

Remove outer leaves and excess stalk from cauliflower and steam until tender. Drain and mash to a purée. Finely chop the onion and fry in butter until soft. Mix mashed cauliflower with onions, breadcrumbs, nutmeg, salt and pepper, sour cream and beaten eggs. Grease a large casserole or soufflé dish and spoon in the cauliflower mixture. Bake at 190°C/375°F/Gas Mark 5 for 1 hour. Sprinkle the top with chopped parsley and serve at once.

Spanish Lentils

Wash lentils and simmer with Marmite and water for half an hour. Add finely chopped vegetables, seasoning, and marjoram. Continue to simmer for about an hour until all the vegetables are cooked and the mixture is fairly thick.

350 g [12 oz] lentils
1½ litres [3 pints] water
2 teaspoons Marmite or yeast
   extract
225 g [8 oz] onions
225 g [8 oz] tomatoes
½ green pepper
2 teaspoons marjoram
salt and pepper

Savoy Gratin

Peel potatoes and simmer in milk until half cooked. Transfer to an open gratin dish retaining just enough milk to come half way up the potatoes. Pour over cream and sprinkle with salt, pepper, nutmeg and Gruyère. Bake at 190°C/375°F/Gas Mark 5 for half an hour.

1½ kg [3 lb] potatoes
50 g [2 oz] Gruyère cheese
250 ml [½ pint] fresh cream
milk
salt and pepper
nutmeg

Chinese Cabbage with Juniper Berries

Wash cabbage and coarsely chop. Simmer with juniper berries in a very little water for 15 minutes. Drain and serve with plenty of black pepper.

900 g [2 lb] Chinese cabbage
1 teaspoon juniper berries
black pepper
water

Lemon Tart

Make pastry by rubbing butter into flour and sugar until it resembles fine breadcrumbs. Bind with an egg. This makes very crumbly pastry. Press into two 20 cm [8 in] flan tins. Melt butter. Remove from heat and add sugar. Whisk in eggs one by one and then add grated rind of 3–4 lemons and whisk in the juice of all of them. Pour into the pastry case and bake at 220°C/425°F/Gas Mark 7 for 40–45 minutes. Leave to cool.

Pastry
225 g [8 oz] plain flour
100 g [4 oz] butter
100 g [4 oz] sugar
1 egg

Filling
100 g [4 oz] butter
325 g [12 oz] sugar
6 eggs
5–6 lemons

Green Pea Soufflé

Glazed Vegetable Pâté and Scrambled Egg
Flan with Pepper Slaw and Potato Salad*

Apricot Cheesecake

Green Pea Soufflé

700 g [1½ lb] frozen peas
3 egg whites
170 ml [7½ fl.oz] double cream
750 ml [1½ pints] water
1 teaspoon Marmite or yeast
  extract
18 g [¾ oz] gelatine or 3
  teaspoons gelozone

Prepare gelatine or gelozone as directed in Chapter 4.
Dissolve Marmite in water and add peas. Bring to the boil
and simmer for 5–8 minutes. Allow to cool and then liquidize. Whisk egg whites and cream separately. Add whipped
cream and dissolved gelatine or gelozone to the pea purée
and mix well. Next fold in the whipped egg whites. Pour
into individual ramekin dishes and chill for 3–4 hours in
the fridge. Serve with brown bread and butter.

Glazed Vegetable Pâté

225 g [8 oz] cooked soya beans
225 g [8 oz] mushrooms
2 medium onions
100 g [4 oz] breadcrumbs
100 g [4 oz] cottage cheese
100 g [4 oz] ground peanuts
1 carrot
4 eggs
½ teaspoon fennel seed
1 teaspoon thyme
garlic salt
1 teaspoon celery seed or salt
black pepper
cooking oil

Glaze
2 teaspoons agar-agar or 12½g
  [½ oz] gelatine
375 ml [¾ pint] water
1 teaspoon Marmite or yeast
  extract
gherkin and bay leaves to garnish

Finely grate carrot and mince mushrooms, onions, breadcrumbs and cottage cheese. Grind soya beans. Mix all ingredients together. Spoon into a large foil-lined loaf tin and
bake in a bain marie at 190°C/375°F/Gas Mark 5 for 1 hour.
Remove foil and allow to cool. Dissolve gelatine and mix
with warm water and Marmite or sprinkle agar-agar over
boiling water and Marmite. Place pâté on large serving
dish and decorate with sliced gherkin and bay leaves. Pour
over the glaze and place in the fridge to set.

* See page 75, multiply quantities by three.

Scrambled Egg Flan

Make pastry by rubbing butter into flour and salt. Bind with a little water. Allow to rest and then roll out to line two 20 cm [8 in] flan cases. Bake blind at 200°C/400°F/Gas Mark 6 for 25–30 minutes. Allow to cool. Scramble the beaten eggs with milk and butter and season to taste. Cook peas and peel and slice tomatoes. Allow all ingredients to cool. Spread scrambled eggs in flan cases and decorate with sliced tomatoes, peas and mint.

Pastry
150 g [6 oz] plain flour
75 g [3 oz] butter
salt
30–45 ml [2–3 tablespoons] water

Filling
12 eggs
25 g [1 oz] butter
125 ml [¼ pint] milk
salt and pepper

Garnish
225 g [8 oz] frozen peas
6 small tomatoes
sprigs of fresh mint

Pepper Slaw

Finely shred cabbage, peppers and gherkins. Toss all ingredients in mayonnaise and add flaked almonds. Season to taste.

½ large white cabbage
2 green peppers
2 red peppers
4 gherkins
2 tablespoons flaked almonds
60 ml [4 tablespoons] mayonnaise
salt and pepper

Apricot Cheesecake

Crush digestive biscuits and mix with melted butter. Bake in a very slow oven 150°C/300°F/Gas Mark 2 for 8 minutes. Allow to cool. Separate egg yolks and beat with cream cheese and sugar. Prepare gelatine or gelozone, as suggested in Chapter 4, and add to mixture. Whip cream and egg whites separately and fold first the cream and then the egg white into the cheese mixture. Pour on to cool base and leave to set. Top with cooked fresh or dried apricots and decorate with flaked almonds.

Base
1½ packets digestive biscuits
150 g [6 oz] butter

Topping
700 g [1½ lb] Philadelphia cheese
3 eggs
225 g [8 oz] sugar
375 ml [¾ pint] double cream
40 g [1½ oz] gelatine or 6
    teaspoons gelozone
1½ kg [3 lb] stewed fresh apricots
    or 700 g [1½ lb] dried apricots
    soaked and puréed
a little water
flaked almonds

Cream of Chick Pea Soup

Mushroom Terrine and Asparagus Cheese with Pickled Vegetables and Toast or French Bread

Strawberry Crunchy Cream

Cream of Chick Pea Soup

450 g [1 lb] chick peas
2 litres [4 pints] vegetable stock
   or water
black pepper
125 ml [$\frac{1}{4}$ pint] double cream
2 egg yolks
fried bread croûtons

Soak chick peas overnight. Drain and place in a pan with stock. Bring to the boil and simmer for $1\frac{1}{2}$ hours until cooked. Rub through a mouli and return to heat. Add black pepper and egg yolks mixed with cream. Reheat but do not boil. Serve with fried bread croûtons.

Mushroom Terrine

700 g [$1\frac{1}{2}$ lb] mushrooms
100 g [4 oz] ground almonds
100 g [4 oz] ground cashew nuts
50 g [2 oz] breadcrumbs
2 eggs
2 onions
1 teaspoon Worcestershire sauce
1 teaspoon garlic salt
2 teaspoons marjoram
2 teaspoons oregano
cooking oil
salt and pepper

Finely chop onions and mushrooms and gently fry until soft. Mix with all other ingredients and spoon into a foil-lined loaf tin or terrine dish. Bake in a bain marie at 180°C/350°F/Gas Mark 4 for 1 hour.

Asparagus Cheese

3 × 175 g [7 oz] (dry weight)
   cans asparagus
350 g [12 oz] cream cheese
150 g [6 oz] butter
salt and pepper

Finely chop or purée asparagus. Melt butter and mix with asparagus and cream cheese. Season to taste and place in fridge to set. Serve with fingers of brown toast or French bread.

Pickled Vegetables

Wash and slice chosen vegetables and parboil in salted water. Drain and simmer in pickling liquor until fully cooked. Allow to cool and serve partially drained.

900 g [2 lb] mixed vegetables:
  cauliflower, celery hearts,
  carrots, beans, leeks,
  aubergines etc.

Pickling Liquor
250 ml [$\frac{1}{2}$ pint] water
250 ml [$\frac{1}{2}$ pint] cider vinegar
125 ml [$\frac{1}{4}$ pint] olive oil
juice of 4 lemons
8 peppercorns
2 cloves
4 bay leaves
2 sprigs thyme
salt

Strawberry Crunchy Cream

Whisk egg white very stiffly and then gradually whisk in half the sugar. Fold in the rest of the sugar, nuts, bicarbonate of soda and essence. Spread meringue about 1 cm [$\frac{1}{2}$ in] thick on rice paper on a baking tray. Bake in a low oven 130°C/250°F/Gas Mark $\frac{1}{2}$ for about 2$\frac{1}{2}$ hours until the meringue is crisp underneath. Leave till cold. Break into pieces. Whip cream until just thick. Halve strawberries and just before serving mix cream, strawberries and meringue pieces in a large bowl.

450 g [1 lb] strawberries
500 ml [1 pint] double cream
2 egg whites
100 g [4 oz] caster sugar
50 g [2 oz] ground walnuts
pinch bicarbonate of soda
vanilla essence

Colombian Onion Soup

**Curried Bean Pie and Cardamom Cheese
Pie with Devonshire Carrots and Turnips
and Creole Potatoes**

Cinnamon Apple Cake

Colombian Onion Soup

1½ kg [3 lb] onions
juice of 1 lemon
water
50 g [2 oz] butter
500 ml [1 pint] vegetable stock
750 ml [1½ pints] milk
2 tablespoons plain flour
white wine
salt and pepper

Peel and slice onions and cover with water and lemon juice. Leave for an hour and then drain well. Fry in butter for 10–15 minutes and add flour and seasoning. Stir well and add milk and stock. Bring to the boil and simmer for 45 minutes. If the soup is too thick, then add a little white wine and correct seasoning.

Curried Bean Pie

Pastry
225 g [8 oz] plain flour
100 g [4 oz] butter
salt water

Filling
450 g [1 lb] haricot beans
4 onions
2 carrots
4 cloves garlic
4 tablespoons plain flour
4 teaspoons cumin seed
2 teaspoons chilli powder
1 teaspoon ginger
8 cardomoms
4 cloves
750 ml [1½ pints] vegetable stock
   or water
cooking oil
salt and pepper

Soak beans overnight in water and drain. Fry finely chopped onion, garlic, carrots and spices in cooking oil for 5 minutes. Add flour and stir well. Then add beans and water and bring to the boil. Simmer till beans are soft and the mixture fairly thick. Allow to cool. Rub fat into flour and salt and mix with water to make the pastry. Roll out and line two 20 cm [8 in] pie dishes. Fill with bean mixture and cover with pastry lids. Fork the edges and prick the centres and bake at 200°C/400°F/Gas Mark 6 for 45 minutes or until the pastry is cooked.

Cardamom Cheese Pie

Rub fat into flour and salt and bind with water. Roll out and line two 20 cm [8 in] pie dishes. Chop hard-boiled eggs and mix with remaining filling ingredients and spoon into pastry bases. Cover with pastry lids. Fork the edges and prick the centre. Bake at 200°C/400°F/Gas Mark 6 for 45 minutes or until the pastry is cooked.

Pastry
225 g [8 oz] plain flour
100 g [4 oz] butter
salt
water

Filling
350 g [12 oz] grated Cheddar
   cheese
225 g [8 oz] raisins
8 hard-boiled eggs
2 tablespoons sugar
2 crushed cardamom seeds

Devonshire Carrots and Turnips

Peel and coarsely chop carrots and turnips. Place in a casserole dish. Dissolve honey in cider and pour over the vegetables. Season and cover. Bake at 200°C/400°F/Gas Mark 6 for 1 hour.

700 g [1½ lb] carrots
700 g [1½ lb] turnips
125 ml [¼ pint] dry cider
1 tablespoon honey
salt and pepper

Creole Potatoes

Peel and slice potatoes and layer with butter, seasoning and tomato paste in a casserole dish. Fill up two thirds of the dish with milk. Cover and bake at 200°C/400°F/Gas Mark 6 for 1 hour.

1½ kg [3 lb] potatoes
2 tablespoons tomato purée
25 g [1 oz] butter
milk
salt and pepper

Cinnamon Apple Cake

Sift the flour into a bowl. Make a hollow in the centre and mix in the salt and water. Flake the fat and add to the mixture. Rub in quickly working from the outside in, to make a smooth dough. Leave to stand in the fridge for 30 minutes.

Grease a loose-bottomed cake tin. Line with the rolled out dough, working the dough up the sides of the tin. Fill with the apple purée. Peel and halve the apples. Core and slice. Place the slices on the purée in circles. Mix the jam with the apricot brandy and spread over the apples. Sprinkle over the almonds. Bake for 30 minutes at 200°C/400°F/Gas Mark 6. Leave to cool and cut into 12 slices.

Base
200 g [7 oz] flour
150 g [6 oz] butter or margarine
30 ml [2 tablespoons] cold water
pinch of salt

Topping
450 g [1 lb] apple purée
   flavoured with 1 teaspoon
   cinnamon
450 g [1 lb] apples
100 g [4 oz] apricot jam
45 ml [3 tablespoons] apricot
   brandy
65 g [2½ oz] split almonds

Ratatouille

Blue Cheese Quiche and Leek and Sesame Flan with Summer Salad and Rice Cake

Chocolate Choux Ring

Ratatouille

450 g [1 lb] tomatoes
450 g [1 lb] courgettes
1 large aubergine
1 green pepper
1 red pepper
3 large onions
2 tablespoons tomato paste
1 tablespoon flour
2 teaspoons oregano
salt and black pepper
cooking oil
125 ml [¼ pint] white wine
chopped parsley

Wash and slice courgettes and onions and dice the other vegetables. Fry onions in cooking oil for 5 minutes and add all other vegetables. Continue to fry gently for 10 minutes. Add remaining ingredients ending with the wine, stir well and bring to the boil. Simmer for 45 minutes, adding more wine if the mixture gets too thick. Leave to cool and serve in individual ramekin dishes topped with freshly chopped parsley.

Blue Cheese Quiche

Pastry
150 g [6 oz] plain flour
75 g [3 oz] butter
salt
30–45 ml [2–3 tablespoons] water

Filling
6 eggs
150 g [6 oz] Cheddar cheese
100 g [4 oz] blue cheese (Danish Blue, Stilton or Roquefort)
250 ml [½ pint] double cream
milk
salt and pepper

Make pastry by rubbing butter into flour and salt. Bind with water. Allow to rest and then roll out to line two 20 cm [8 in] flan cases. Grate Cheddar cheese and mix with beaten eggs, cream and a little milk. Season and pour half the mixture into each flan. If the mixture is a little sparse add a little more milk and fork in taking care not to pierce the pastry. Place on tray and bake at 200°C/400°F/Gas Mark 6 for ½ hour. Top each flan with grated blue cheese and return to the oven for a further 20 minutes or until cooked through. Leave to cool.

Stuffed Avocados in Tomato Sauce (page 121), Duchesse Potatoes (page 122) and Cauliflower Almandine (page 121)

Overleaf, left: Greek Salad (page 92); right: Orange Cheese Truffles (page 158), Pinwheels (page 156), Stuffed Dates (page 157), Mali Canapés (page 158) and Cucumber Crowns (page 157)

Leek and Sesame Flan

Make pastry by rubbing butter into flour and salt. Bind with water. Allow to rest and then roll out to line two 20 cm [8 in] flan cases. Steam leeks in a very little water till cooked. Drain well and leave to cool. Place in the base of the flan cases and sprinkle with sesame seeds and salt and pepper. Grate cheese and mix with beaten eggs and cream. Pour over the leeks. If the flans need to be a little fuller add some milk and mix in with a fork taking care not to pierce the pastry. Bake at 200°C/400°F/Gas Mark 6 for 1 hour or until the flan is golden all over the top and the centre is cooked through. Leave to cool.

Pastry
150 g [6 oz] plain flour
75 g [3 oz] butter
salt
30–45 ml [2–3 tablespoons] water

Filling
700 g [1½ lb] leeks
150 g [6 oz] Cheddar cheese
6 eggs
250 ml [½ pint] double cream
milk
salt and pepper
1 teaspoon toasted ground
    sesame seeds

Summer Salad

Mix French mustard, sugar and seasoning into oil and vinegar. Mix all other ingredients together and pour over the dressing.

450 g [1 lb] fresh new peas
450 g [1 lb] finely sliced new
    green beans
10 cm [4 in] cucumber, diced
1 diced green pepper
125 ml [¼ pint] oil and vinegar
    dressing
2 teaspoons French mustard
1 teaspoon sugar
salt and pepper

Rice Cake

Cook the rice in boiling salted water. Drain well and dry over a low heat or in the oven. Leave to cool. Grate the beetroot and mix with peanuts and chopped hard boiled eggs. Then add the cream and stir well. Pack into a loaf tin and weight the top. Chill well and serve garnished with watercress.

450 g [1 lb] rice
225 g [8 oz] cooked beetroot
250 ml [½ pint] sour cream
4 hard-boiled eggs
75 g [3 oz] roasted peanuts
salt and pepper
watercress

Plum Cheesecake (page 115)

Chocolate Choux Ring

Choux pastry
225 g [8 oz] plain flour
500 ml [1 pint] water
100 g [4 oz] butter
2 egg yolks
4 eggs
¼ teaspoon salt
1 teaspoon vanilla essence

Filling
500 ml [1 pint] cream
150 g [6 oz] sugar
200 ml [8 fl.oz] cocoa

Topping
225 g [8 oz] icing sugar
75 g [3 oz] plain chocolate
125 ml [¼ pint] water

Place water, salt and butter in a pan and bring to the boil. Add flour and beat well to a smooth paste that leaves the sides of the pan clean. Remove from heat and add egg yolks and vanilla. Beat well and add the remaining eggs one by one beating all the time. Grease a baking tray and pipe two rings of choux pastry on to it. Bake at 220°C/425°F/Gas Mark 7 until the choux ring is risen and crisp. Continue cooking until the centres are dry and the outside fairly brown. Place on a cooling tray and slit round the outside of the rings about halfway up. Leave to cool. Meanwhile make cocoa with boiling water, to the normal strength and leave to cool. Whip cold cocoa with sugar and cream and use this mixture to fill the centres of the rings. Make the topping by breaking the chocolate into small pieces and placing in a bowl over warm water. Allow to dissolve. Add icing sugar and water and stir until well mixed and smooth. Spread over the top of each ring and serve when the icing is set.

Apple and Celery Soup

Mali Pie and Artichoke and Egg Flan, Sprouts with Nutmeg and Potatoes Provençale

Apricots in Ginger

Apple and Celery Soup

25 g [1 oz] butter
3 onions
3 sherry glasses sherry
700 g [1½ lb] cooking apples
700 g [1½ lb] celery
1¾ litres [3¾ pints] water
2 teaspoons cumin
salt and pepper
125 ml [¼ pint] sour cream
ratafia biscuits

Melt butter in pan and fry chopped onion. Add sherry and bring to the boil. Next add chopped apples and celery and water. Sprinkle with cumin and seasoning and bring to the boil. Simmer for 45 minutes and pass through mouli. Add sour cream and reheat before serving. Do not boil. Serve garnished with small ratafia biscuits.

Mali Pie

Fry onions in cooking oil for 10 minutes until soft and brown. Stir in peanuts, tomatoes, Worcestershire sauce, herbs and seasoning. Boil for 2–3 minutes to reduce tomato juice if necessary. Leave to cool. Meanwhile rub fat into flour to make pastry and bind with water. Roll out and line two 20 cm [8 in] pie dishes. Place half the peanut mixture in each pie and cover with a pastry crust. Fork the edges and prick the centre. Bake at 200°C/400°F/Gas Mark 6 for about 45 minutes or until the pastry is cooked.

Pastry
225 g [8 oz] plain flour
100 g [4 oz] butter
salt
water

Filling
350 g [12 oz] onions
350 g [12 oz] ground roast
 peanuts
1 large tin tomatoes or 12 fresh
 tomatoes
2 tablespoons marjoram
2 teaspoons Worcestershire sauce
cooking oil

Artichoke and Egg Flan

Make pastry by rubbing fat into flour and salt. Bind with a little water. Allow to rest and then roll out to line two 20 cm [8 in] flan cases. Bake blind for 8–10 minutes. Remove from oven and cover base with sliced artichoke hearts and cottage cheese. Season very well. Beat eggs with milk and pour over the top. Bake at 200°C/400°F/Gas Mark 6 for an hour until the flan is set and slightly browned.

Pastry
150 g [6 oz] plain flour
75 g [3 oz] butter
salt
water

Filling
12 artichoke hearts
225 g [8 oz] cottage cheese
4 eggs
250 ml [$\frac{1}{2}$ pint] milk
salt and pepper

Sprouts with Nutmeg

Remove outside leaves of sprouts and steam or simmer in salted water. Drain and dot with butter. Sprinkle with nutmeg and serve.

$1\frac{1}{2}$ kg [3 lb] sprouts
water
nutmeg
salt
butter

Potatoes Provençale

Melt butter with oil in a large frying pan. Fry finely chopped garlic and diced potatoes in the fat till soft. Serve sprinkled with chopped parsley.

$1\frac{1}{2}$ kg [3 lb] potatoes
2 cloves garlic
2 tablespoons parsley
25 g [1 oz] butter
45 ml [3 tablespoons] cooking oil

Apricots in Ginger

900 g [2 lb] dried apricots
375 ml [¾ pint] ginger wine
500 ml [1 pint] white wine
water

Wash apricots well and soak overnight in 250 ml [½ pint] of ginger wine, white wine and enough water to cover. Pour into a large pan and bring to the boil. Simmer for 20–30 minutes until apricots are cooked but not falling apart. Allow to cool and transfer to a glass dish. Top with remaining 125 ml [¼ pint] ginger wine and serve with fresh cream.

Senegal Eggs

Lancashire Cheese Log with Pasta Salad, Grape and Fennel Salad and American Corn Bread

Avocado Chartreuse

Senegal Eggs

12 hard-boiled eggs
4 tablespoons peanut butter
3 oranges
1 sliced orange for garnish
1 bunch watercress

Halve hard-boiled eggs and arrange on a large plate. Mix peanut butter with juice of three oranges and a little orange rind. Add a little water if the mixture is too thick. It should pour easily over the eggs. Garnish with orange slices and watercress round the edge of the plate.

Lancashire Cheese Log

700 g [1½ lb] Lancashire cheese
6 small gherkins
8 stuffed olives
1 tablespoon chopped chives
1 teaspoon thyme
1 teaspoon French mustard
salt and black pepper
90 ml [6 tablespoons]
    mayonnaise
a little single cream
lettuce

Finely chop gherkins and olives and mix all ingredients together. Bind with mayonnaise and a little cream to make a stiffish mixture. Shape into two rolls and wrap in grease-proof paper. Chill and serve sliced on a bed of lettuce.

Pasta Salad

Cook pasta in boiling, salted water for about 20 minutes. Drain and allow to cool. Shred pepper and chop apple and celery. Mix all ingredients together and sprinkle with marjoram.

225 g [8 oz] mixed pasta shapes
100 g [4 oz] cooked soya beans
½ green pepper
1 apple
3 sticks celery
45 ml [3 tablespoons] oil and vinegar dressing
marjoram
salt and pepper

Grape and Fennel Salad

Parboil sliced fennel for 5 minutes. Drain and leave to cool. Halve and stone grapes and mix with chopped fennel. Add sour cream and salt and pepper and garnish with mint.

3 large fennel hearts
450 g [1 lb] green grapes
125 ml [¼ pint] sour cream
salt and pepper
2 sprigs of mint

American Corn Bread

Beat eggs and milk together and dissolve honey in the mixture. Add oil and pour over the dry ingredients. Stir well and pour into two well greased 20 × 20 cm [8 × 8 in] square tins and bake in a moderate oven for about an hour.

275 g [10 oz] polenta or yellow corn meal
150 g [6 oz] plain flour
90 ml [6 tablespoons] corn oil
4 tablespoons honey
2 eggs
400 ml [16 fl.oz] milk
2 teaspoons salt
4 teaspoons baking powder

Avocado Chartreuse

Whip 625 ml [1¼ pints] of double cream with sugar and Chartreuse until stiff. Peel and stone avocados and sieve quickly into cream mixture. Stir well and pour into individual dishes. Decorate with angelica and a little more whipped cream and serve as soon as possible as the avocado has a slight tendency to discolour.

6 avocados
750 ml [1½ pints] double cream
6 tablespoons sugar or honey
3 miniature bottles Green Chartreuse
angelica

Beanshoot Salad with Cream Cheese
Dressing

Mexican Baked Spinach with Jollof Rice
and Aubergine Corn

Hazelnut Ice Cream with Poached Pears

Beanshoot Salad with Cream Cheese Dressing

350 g [12 oz] beanshoots
100 g [4 oz] mushrooms
　(smallish)
1 green pepper
½ cucumber
1 bunch watercress

Dressing
225 g [8 oz] cream cheese
90 ml [6 tablespoons] milk
4 tablespoons chopped parsley

Dice cucumber, mushrooms and green pepper and mix with all other ingredients. Season. To make dressing mix cream cheese with milk until fairly runny. Add chopped parsley to dressing. Season to taste. Chill and pour over the salad. Serve at once.

Mexican Baked Spinach

2¾ kg [6 lbs] spinach
4 green peppers
2 large onions
½ head celery
100 g [4 oz] raisins
1 teaspoon cinnamon
½ teaspoon Cayenne pepper
½ teaspoon dill seed
125 ml [¼ pint] tomato juice
225 g [8 oz] grated cheese
salt and pepper
cooking oil

Wash spinach and steam in a large pan for 5 minutes until the size is reduced considerably. Slice green peppers and blanch for 5 minutes in boiling water. Finely chop onions and celery and fry in cooking oil with cinnamon, Cayenne pepper and dill seed for 5 minutes. Place half the spinach in the base of a large oval earthenware dish. Add a layer of peppers and then all the onion and celery mixture. Sprinkle with half the cheese and cover with remaining peppers. Next add remaining spinach and top with grated cheese. Sprinkle each layer with seasoning as you go. Bake at 190°C/375°F/Gas Mark 5 for 45 minutes.

Jollof Rice

Finely chop onions and sauté in cooking oil till soft and beginning to brown. Add rice and continue to cook for 10 minutes, stirring from time to time. Stir in raisins, tin of tomatoes, seasoning and stock. Cook for about 30 minutes until rice is tender and the liquid just absorbed. Add peanuts and cook for a further 5 minutes, stirring from time to time.

350 g [12 oz] rice
450 g [1 lb] onions
100 g [4 oz] roast peanuts
50 g [2 oz] raisins or sultanas
450 g [1 lb] tin tomatoes
250 ml [$\frac{1}{2}$ pint] vegetable stock
$\frac{1}{4}$ teaspoon Cayenne pepper
$\frac{1}{4}$ teaspoon salt
cooking oil

Aubergine Corn

Slice aubergines in rings and sauté in cooking oil. Layer in a casserole with corn and peeled tomatoes, seasoning each layer as you go. Sprinkle with breadcrumbs and dot with butter. Bake at 190°C/375°F/Gas Mark 5 for 45 minutes.

6 medium aubergines
2 large tins mexicorn
450 g [1 lb] tomatoes
100 g [4 oz] breadcrumbs
butter
salt and pepper
cooking oil

Hazelnut Ice Cream

Whisk eggs with runny honey till thick and pale in colour. Whip milk and cream until really stiff. Add ground hazelnuts quickly and fold in the egg mixture. Pour into container and freeze. To serve spoon into individual dishes and sprinkle with grated chocolate.

9 eggs
3 tablespoons runny honey
375 ml [$\frac{3}{4}$ pint] double cream
250 ml [$\frac{1}{2}$ pint] milk
150 g [6 oz] ground hazelnuts
1 small bar plain chocolate

Poached Pears

Peel, halve and core pears and poach gently in white wine and honey for 20 minutes. Allow to cool and chill slightly before serving.

6 Conference pears
125 ml [$\frac{1}{4}$ pint] white wine
1 tablespoon honey

New England Jellied Vegetables

Savoury Herb Quiche, Oat, Cheese and Tomato Flan with Cauliflower Salad and Sweetcorn and Watercress Salad

Gaelic Coffee Ice Cream Gâteau

New England Jellied Vegetables

275 g [10 oz] tin cut asparagus
400 g [14 oz] tin celery
2 hard-boiled eggs
4 cooked and peeled new
    potatoes
2 large gherkins
4 stuffed olives
2 teaspoons agar-agar or 12½ g
    [½ oz] gelatine
750 ml [¾ pint] water
1 teaspoon Marmite or yeast
    extract
parsley

Slice eggs and vegetables. Dissolve gelatine and mix with warm water and Marmite or sprinkle agar-agar over boiling water and Marmite. Allow to cool but not to set. Pour a little of the mixture into a gratin dish and place in fridge to set. Arrange the egg, olives and gherkins on the jelly base and arrange the remaining vegetables and egg on top. Cover with the rest of the jelly and place in fridge to set. Alternatively arrange the eggs and vegetables in individual ramekin dishes and set the jelly in these. Turn out to serve and decorate with parsley.

Savoury Herb Quiche

Pastry
150 g [6 oz] plain flour
75 g [3 oz] butter
salt
water

Filling
6 eggs
225 g [8 oz] Cheddar cheese
250 ml [½ pint] double cream
125 ml [¼ pint] milk
½ teaspoon each of thyme,
    tarragon, marjoram, basil
1 tablespoon freshly chopped
    parsley
salt and black pepper

Make pastry by rubbing butter into flour and salt. Bind with water. Allow to rest and then roll out to line two 20 cm [8 in] flan cases. Grate cheese and mix with beaten eggs, cream and milk. Add herbs and seasoning and pour half the mixture into each flan case. Bake at 200°C/400°F/Gas Mark 6 for about an hour until golden brown on top and cooked through the centre. Allow to cool.

Oat, Cheese and Tomato Flan

Make pastry by rubbing butter into flour, salt and oats. Bind with a little water. Press into two 20 cm [8 in] flan cases. Finely chop onions and fry in cooking oil until transparent. Mix with nuts, cheese, tomato paste, seasoning and beaten eggs and fill each flan case. Bake at 200°C/400°F/Gas Mark 6 for about 45 minutes. Allow to cool.

Pastry
100 g [4 oz] butter
100 g [4 oz] rolled oats
100 g [4 oz] plain flour
water
salt

Filling
4 large onions
225 g [8 oz] grated Edam cheese
100 g [4 oz] ground hazelnuts
4 tablespoons tomato paste
60 ml [4 tablespoons] double cream
3 eggs
salt and pepper
cooking oil

Cauliflower Salad

Clean the cauliflowers and discard the stems. Divide into florets and immerse in oil and vinegar dressing. Leave for 2 hours. Finely chop other ingredients and mix with drained cauliflower, orange juice and black pepper. Serve in a bowl lined with lettuce.

2 small young cauliflowers
125 ml [$\frac{1}{4}$ pint] oil and vinegar dressing
1 head celery
2 red peppers
4 large gherkins
1 onion
juice of 2 oranges
black pepper
1 lettuce

Sweetcorn and Watercress Salad

Coarsely chop washed and drained watercress and mix with drained sweetcorn. Toss in dressing and sprinkle with black pepper.

3 bunches watercress
2 × 175 g [7 oz] tins mexicorn
45 ml [3 tablespoons] oil and vinegar dressing
black pepper

Gaelic Coffee Ice Cream Gâteau

Coffee Ice Cream
250 ml [½ pint] double cream
100 g [4 oz] Barbados or
   molasses sugar
150 ml [5 fl.oz] coffee made with
   1½ tablespoons instant coffee

Gaelic Ice Cream
250 ml [½ pint] double cream
1 tablespoon honey
60 ml [4 tablespoons] whisky

Decoration
125 ml [¼ pint] double cream
flaked almonds

Whip cream, coffee and sugar until as stiff as it will go. Dissolve honey in whisky and whisk with cream until as stiff as possible. Place half the coffee mixture in a square solid-based cake tin and place in freezer. When set cover with half the gaelic ice cream mixture and return to freezer. Follow up with another layer of each freezing between each addition. If the cream mixtures start to separate before they are added to the layer cake, rewhip. Freeze cake. Just before serving decorate with whipped cream and flaked almonds.

Melon and Avocado Salad

Borlotti Vegetable Casserole with Tarragon Rice and Red Cabbage Salad

Rhubarb and Walnut Ginger Crumble

Melon and Avocado Salad

1 honeydew melon
4 large avocados
1 bunch watercress

Dressing
juice of 3 lemons
125 ml [¼ pint] corn oil
1 tablespoon freshly chopped
   mint
black pepper

Mix dressing ingredients. Peel and cube melon and avocados and mix with dressing immediately to prevent discolouration of the avocados. Chill for 30 minutes and serve in individual bowls with a little watercress.

Tarragon Rice

800 g [1 lb 12 oz] rice
1 tablespoon tarragon
salt
water
butter

Cook rice in boiling salted water until tender. Drain well and mix with tarragon. Serve dotted with knobs of butter.

Borlotti Vegetable Casserole

Soak Borlotti beans overnight. Finely slice onion and fry in cooking oil in a large pan until it starts to turn transparent. Add flour and continue cooking for 2–3 minutes, stirring all the time. Gradually add vegetable stock, still stirring, and bring to the boil. Add beans, herbs, seasoning and Marmite. Simmer for 45 minutes. Peel and slice carrots, wash and slice celery, and wash and separate cauliflower florets. Add to the beans with parsley, white wine and sufficient water to just about cover the vegetables with the sauce. Bring back to the boil and simmer for another $\frac{1}{2}$–$\frac{3}{4}$ hour until all the beans and vegetables are cooked through. Correct seasoning and serve.

350 g [12 oz] dried Borlotti beans
6 onions
6 tablespoons plain flour
1$\frac{1}{2}$ litres [3 pints] vegetable stock
2 teaspoons Marmite or yeast extract
cooking oil
2 teaspoons celery seed or salt
1 teaspoon tarragon
2 teaspoon marjoram
black pepper
350 g [12 oz] shelled broad beans
6 carrots
1 head celery
1 cauliflower
300 ml [12 fl.oz] white wine
300 ml [12 fl.oz] water
3 tablespoons chopped parsley

Red Cabbage Salad

Finely shred red cabbage and mix with very finely chopped celery and onion. Toss in dressing and season to taste.

1 red cabbage
4 sticks celery
1 small onion
90 ml [6 tablespoons] oil and vinegar dressing
salt and pepper

Rhubarb and Walnut Ginger Crumble

Wash and chop rhubarb and place in a pan with sugar or honey, lemon juice and sufficient water to cover about two thirds of the rhubarb. Bring to the boil and simmer for 10 minutes or until the rhubarb is soft. Make the crumble topping by rubbing the fat into the flour and mixing with nuts, sugar and ginger. Place rhubarb in a large oval dish and sprinkle on the crumble, pressing down lightly. Bake at 180°C/350°F/Gas Mark 4 for about 40–45 minutes until golden brown.

1$\frac{1}{2}$ kg [3 lb] rhubarb
6 tablespoons Barbados sugar or honey
juice of 1 lemon
100 g [4 oz] raisins

Topping
400 g [14 oz] plain flour
225 g [8 oz] butter or margarine
225 g [8 oz] sugar
100 g [4 oz] chopped walnuts
$\frac{1}{2}$ teaspoon ground ginger

12 Catering for a Cocktail Party

This chapter includes canapés, dips and hot savouries. The recipes are all for 24 people, given a selection of five or six items for the party.

The canapés are served cold, arranged on decorative plates or on savoury doyleys either mixed or separately.

The dips should be served in bowls surrounded by smaller bowls of crudités, small cheese biscuits and crisps. Crudités would include long, slim wedges of carrot, cucumber, celery and spring onions as well as cauliflower florets and olives.

The savouries are all served hot with cocktail sticks to handle them.

Canapés

Pinwheels

8 large slices bread
350 g [12 oz] cream cheese
60 ml [4 tablespoons] single cream
2 teaspoons toasted ground sesame seeds
2 teaspoons rosemary
salt and pepper

Mix cream cheese with sufficient cream to give a smooth, thick, creamy consistency. Divide into two batches and mix one with sesame seeds and the other with rosemary. Season each batch to taste. Spread thinly sliced bread that has had its crusts removed with the cream cheese mixtures. Roll up lengthways and slice into six pinwheels per slice.

Cucumber Crowns

1 large cucumber
6 eggs
24 stuffed olives
paprika pepper

Slice cucumber into 48 rounds. Hard boil and slice eggs. Halve stuffed olives. Arrange cucumber on a large plate and place a slice of egg on each piece. Top with half a stuffed olive and sprinkle with paprika pepper.

Almond and Onion Pâté Savouries

Chop onions as finely as possible and gently fry in a little of the butter until soft and lightly browned. Mix with remaining butter until smooth and runny. Add almonds, herbs and seasoning and spoon into a dish. Leave to set. Spread on to rounds of toast and cut each round into eight.

6 large slices toast
3 onions
75 g [3 oz] butter
125 g [5 oz] ground almonds
1 teaspoon celery seed
1 teaspoon summer savory
salt and pepper

Curried Bean and Onion Squares

Finely chop onions and fry in cooking oil with curry powder, ground cumin and garlic salt until transparent. Add water and continue to simmer for 5–8 minutes. Add ground cooked soya beans and mix well. Allow to cool and spread on fried bread. Cut into squares and serve sprinkled with freshly chopped parsley.

7–8 large slices fried bread
225 g [8 oz] cooked soya beans
4 small onions
1½ teaspoons curry powder
2 teaspoons ground cumin seed
3 teaspoons garlic salt
60 ml [4 tablespoons] water
cooking oil
chopped parsley

Stuffed Dates

Mix cream cheese with mayonnaise and add sesame seeds and seasoning. Stone dates and fill with cream cheese mixture. Push a stuffed olive or a quarter walnut into the centre of each date.

48 dates
125 g [5 oz] cream cheese
1 teaspoon toasted ground
    sesame seeds
10–15 ml [2–3 teaspoons]
    mayonnaise
salt and pepper
24 stuffed olives
24 walnut quarters

Peanut Cheese Squares

Rub fat into flour and salt and then mix in the grated cheese with a fork. The mixture should form a very stiff paste. Roll out to ½ cm [¼ in] thick. Brush with beaten egg and sprinkle with chopped peanuts. Cut into small squares and bake for 15 minutes at 190°C/375°F/Gas Mark 5. Remove from tin and allow to cool on a wire rack.

100 g [4 oz] plain flour
100 g [4 oz] butter
100 g [4 oz] grated Cheddar
    cheese

Mali Canapés

8 rounds toast
100 g [4 oz] grated Cheddar
   cheese
50 g [2 oz] roasted peanuts
25 g [1 oz] chopped raisins
30 ml [2 tablespoons]
   mayonnaise
salt and pepper

Mix all ingredients together with mayonnaise to bind. Chill for an hour and then spread onto rounds of toast. Cut each piece into six squares and serve sprinkled with chopped parsley.

Camembert Canapés

Pastry
200 g [7 oz] flour
100 g [4 oz] dry curd cheese
100 g [4 oz] butter
salt
1 egg yolk
caraway seeds

Filling
125 g [5 oz] ripe Camembert
   cheese
50 g [2 oz] butter
1 small onion
1 small gherkin
$\frac{1}{2}$ teaspoon paprika
salt
parsley
$\frac{1}{2}$ teaspoon dried dill

Crumble the curd cheese into flour and salt lightly. Flake the butter and add to the flour. Rub in well to make a smooth dough. Wrap in greaseproof paper and leave in the fridge for 30 minutes. Roll out the dough on a floured board to about $\frac{1}{4}$ in thick. Cut into rings with a pastry cutter (approximately 90 rings), 3.5 cm [$1\frac{1}{2}$ in] in diameter. Glaze half the rings with the beaten egg yolk and sprinkle on the caraway seeds. Put all the dough rings on a baking tray and bake for 15 minutes at 200°C/400°F/Gas Mark 6.

Meanwhile put the Camembert in a bowl and mash with a fork. Beat in the softened butter and mix to a smooth cream. Season with salt and paprika. Peel the onion and chop finely. Chop the gherkin and parsley. Mix these and the dill into the creamy mixture. Wrap in greaseproof paper and leave in the freezer compartment of the fridge for 20 minutes. Spread the unglazed half of the dough rings with the cheese mixture and cover with the glazed halves.

Orange Cheese Truffles

450 g [1 lb] soft cream cheese
225 g [8 oz] dates
225 g [8 oz] raisins
150 g [6 oz] flaked almonds
30 ml [2 tablespoons] orange
   juice
1 teaspoon mixed spice
3–4 tablespoons toasted ground
   sesame seeds
7 oranges

Finely chop dates, raisins and almonds and mix with cream cheese. Add grated rind of one orange and mixed spice with enough orange juice to make a stiff paste. Mix well and chill for 4–6 hours. Remove from fridge and shape into about 100 small balls. Roll in toasted ground sesame seeds. Slice remaining oranges in slim wedges and arrange on a large plate with the cheese truffles.

Mixed Cheese Puffs

Melt butter or margarine in water and bring to the boil. Beat in flour and salt with a wooden spoon until the mixture forms a smooth ball of dough. Remove from heat and beat in the eggs one by one. Using a forcing bag fitted with a 1 cm [½ in] plain nozzle, pipe small balls onto a lightly greased baking tray. Bake at 190°C/375°F/Gas Mark 5 for 30 minutes. Leave to cool. Mix cream cheese with sour cream and divide in two. Add sesame seeds to one half and mixed herbs to the other. When the choux puffs are cool, make a small hole and fill with flavoured cheese.

350 g [10 oz] plain flour
pinch of salt
225 g [8 oz] butter
7–8 eggs
500 ml [1 pint] water

Filling
450 g [1 lb] cream cheese
125 ml [¼ pint] sour cream
1–2 tablespoons toasted ground sesame seeds
1–2 tablespoons mixed chopped herbs

Dips

Indian Curry Dip

Soak chick peas in water overnight and drain well. Fry onion, garlic and spices in butter until onions start to soften. Add chick peas and flour and stir well. Add water and bring to the boil. Simmer for 1½–2 hours until the peas are soft. Allow to cool and pass through a mouli. Mix with cream cheese and milk to form a smooth creamy paste. Add more curry powder to taste.

150 g [6 oz] chick peas
1 onion
1 tablespoon flour
2 cloves garlic
1 piece stem ginger
2 green chillis without seeds
1 teaspoon turmeric
½ teaspoon coriander
25 g [1 oz] butter
375 ml [¾ pint] water
salt and pepper
350 g [12 oz] cream cheese
150 ml [6 fl.oz] milk
½ teaspoon curry powder, optional

Garlic Dip

Crush garlic in a little salt and add to mayonnaise. Add lemon juice and plenty of black pepper to taste.

225 g [8 oz] mayonnaise
4 cloves garlic
juice of 1 lemon
black pepper
salt

Mexican Dip

450 g [1 lb] tin Lima beans
½ green pepper
1 small onion
1 tablespoon tomato paste
75 ml [3 fl.oz] cream
150 ml [6 fl.oz] tomato juice
juice of half a lemon
10–15 ml [2–3 teaspoons]
    Worcestershire sauce
paprika
garlic salt
black pepper
cooking oil

Fry coarsely chopped onion and green pepper in cooking oil until fairly soft. Drain beans and pass through a mouli with the onion and pepper. Add all other ingredients and mix to a smooth creamy paste.

Sesame and Chutney Dip

450 g [1 lb] cream cheese
3 tablespoons blended chutney
1 tablespoon toasted ground
    sesame seeds
salt and pepper
a little milk

Blend all ingredients with a fork, adding a little more milk if necessary to give a creamy consistency.

Peanut Dip

450 g [1 lb] cream cheese
150 ml [6 fl.oz] milk
4 tablespoons peanut butter
30 ml [2 tablespoons] cream

Blend all ingredients with a fork, adding milk gradually to achieve a smooth creamy consistency.

Chick Pea and Sesame Dip

700 g [1½ lb] chick peas
375 g [13 oz] sesame seeds
250 ml [½ pint] salad oil
12 lemons
4 cloves garlic
4 tablespoons finely chopped
    parsley
Greek bread

Cook chick peas (see Chapter 4). Rub through a sieve and mix with ground sesame seeds. Add lemon juice and crushed cloves of garlic. Stir in the salad oil just before serving and sprinkle with chopped parsley. Serve with small pieces of hot Greek bread.

Egg and Avocado Dip

Peel and mash avocados. Add lemon juice and mayonnaise. Peel, de-seed and chop tomatoes and finely chop or sieve eggs and add to the mixture. Season to taste and serve on a bed of lettuce, sprinkled with paprika pepper.

5 avocados
12 hard-boiled eggs
6 tomatoes
90 ml [6 tablespoons] lemon juice
90 ml [6 tablespoons] mayonnaise
paprika pepper
salt and pepper
3–4 lettuce leaves

Artichoke Dip

Sieve the artichoke hearts and mix with lemon juice. Stir in mayonnaise and season to taste.

12 artichoke hearts
225 g [8 oz] mayonnaise
juice of 1 lemon
salt and pepper

Savouries

Spiced Lentil Tartlets

Fry finely chopped onion with garlic and spices for 5 minutes. Wash lentils and add to onions. Cover with water and add all other filling ingredients. Bring to the boil and simmer until the lentils are cooked and the mixture is fairly thick, about 1–1½ hours. Meanwhile rub fat into flour and salt and bind with water. Roll out fairly thinly and line 24 small tartlet tins with pastry. Place a spoonful of cold filling in each tartlet and cover with a pastry lid. Bake at 200°C/400°F/Gas Mark 6 for about 35–40 minutes until the pastry is beginning to brown. Serve hot.

Pastry
225 g [8 oz] plain flour
100 g [4 oz] butter
salt
water

Filling
100 g [4 oz] lentils
500 ml [1 pint] water
1 teaspoon Marmite or yeast extract
1 large onion
1 clove garlic
1 tablespoon tomato paste
½ teaspoon chilli powder
¼ teaspoon ground cumin seed
½ teaspoon thyme
¼ teaspoon allspice
salt and pepper
cooking oil

Camembert Gems

450 g [1 lb] Camembert
100 g [4 oz] flour
100 g [4 oz] butter
625 ml [1¼ pints] milk
2 teaspoons tarragon
salt and pepper
3 eggs
100–150 g [4–6 oz] fine
  breadcrumbs

Make a thick roux with the flour, butter and milk and add grated Camembert, tarragon and seasoning. Allow to cool with greaseproof paper over the top. Spoon out small balls and roll in egg and then in breadcrumbs and deep fry. Do not leave in the fat too long or the cheese will cause the balls to run. For a milder taste use Brie cheese.

Cheese Dreams

12 slices bread
450 g [1 lb] grated cheese
4 tablespoons chutney
salt and pepper
butter

Butter bread and mix cheese and chutney. Make up six sandwiches with the bread and the cheese mixture. Cut each sandwich into quarters and each quarter into a triangle. Fry each triangle on both sides in hot butter and serve at once.

Cheesy Courgette Bites

8 large slices buttered bread
3–4 courgettes
225 g [8 oz] grated cheese
1 teaspoon oregano
salt and pepper
4 eggs
cooking oil

Cook courgettes and mash. Allow to cool and mix with grated cheese, oregano and seasoning. Spread on to four slices of bread and top with remaining four slices. Cut each sandwich into 12 bite-sized squares, dip in beaten egg and fry quickly on both sides in cooking oil. Serve at once.

Savoury Nut Balls

50 g [2 oz] plain flour
50 g [2 oz] butter
100 g [4 oz] ground hazelnuts
25 g [1 oz] buckwheat flour
1 teaspoon oregano
250 ml [½ pint] milk
salt and pepper
50 g [2 oz] dried breadcrumbs
1 beaten egg

Make a thick roux with flour, butter and milk and add buckwheat flour. Continue cooking for 5 minutes. Add hazelnuts, herbs and seasoning and allow to cool. Shape into small bite-sized balls and roll in beaten egg and then in breadcrumbs. Deep fry and serve at once.

Bibliography

Manual of Nutrition, Ministry of Agriculture, Fisheries and Food, HMSO.

The Facts of Food, Arnold E. Bender, Oxford University Press.

Let's Eat Right To Keep Fit, Adelle Davis, Unwin Paperbacks.

The Loaf and the Law, Kenneth Barlow, Precision Press.

Eating Your Way to Health, Ruth Bircher, Faber and Faber Ltd.

Diet For a Small Planet, Frances Moore Lappe, Ballantine Books (New York).

Nutrition: Better Health through Good Eating, Sheila Bingham, Corgi Paperbacks.

'Repair function of cholesterol versus the lipid theory of arteriosclerosis', Hans Kaunitz, *Chemistry and Industry*, 17 September 1977.

'Diet-Heart: End of an Era', George V. Mann, *New England Journal of Medicine*, September 22, 1977.

'Your Diet and your Heart', Sir John McMichael, *Home Economics*, November 1977.

'Arteriosclerosis – a cause for concern', Dr Malcolm Parry, *Home Economics*, April 1978.

Index